To Brad, w̶ me in pers. ∂ W9-ALT-451 ̶ ̶ ̶ ̶.

Peter

God's Mercy Revealed

Healing for a Broken World

Peter Magee

PeteraMagee
05/29/05

SERVANT BOOKS

PUBLISHED BY ST. ANTHONY MESSENGER PRESS
CINCINNATI, OHIO

Scripture passages have been taken from the *New Revised Standard Version Bible,* copyright ©1989 by the Division of Christian Education of the National Council of the Churches of Christ in the U.S.A., and used by permission. All rights reserved.

Cover design by Candle Light Studios
Book design by Phillips Robinette, O.F.M.

Library of Congress Cataloging-in-Publication Data

Magee, Peter, 1958-
  God's mercy revealed : healing for a broken world / Peter Magee.
     p. cm.
  ISBN 0-86716-656-8 (pbk. : alk. paper)
  1. God—Mercy—Meditations. 2. Christian life—Catholic authors. 3. Catholic Church—Prayer-books and devotions—English. I. Title.
  BT153.M4M34 2005
  231'.6—dc22

                        2005005120
ISBN 0-86716-656-8

Published by Servant Books, an imprint of St. Anthony Messenger Press.
28 W. Liberty St.
Cincinnati, OH 45202
www.AmericanCatholic.org

Printed in the United States of America
Printed on acid-free paper

05 06 07 08 09 10 9 8 7 6 5 4 3 2 1

Contents

Foreword by Archbishop Gabriel Montalvo / v

Introduction / vii

PART ONE: MERCY AND THE TRINITY

Chapter One: Being and Giving Forgiveness / 2

Chapter Two: The Forlorn Father / 10

Chapter Three: Spirit-Driven / 18

Chapter Four: Remembering the Healer / 25

Chapter Five: Questions of the Merciful One / 33

Chapter Six: Exalt the Cross of Mercy / 42

PART TWO: MERCY AND THE CHURCH

Chapter Seven: Prophet of Mercy / 52

Chapter Eight: The Cleansed Temple of Mercy / 59

Chapter Nine: Mercifully Catholic / 68

PART THREE: MERCY AND THE SACRAMENTS

Chapter Ten: Be Opened! / 78

Chapter Eleven: The Body of Merciful Love / 84

Chapter Twelve: The Bread and Breath of Life / 90

Chapter Thirteen: Divine Mercy / 95

PART FOUR: MERCY AND LIFE

Chapter Fourteen: From the Bottom of the Heart / 106

Chapter Fifteen: Attractive Distractions / 114

Chapter Sixteen: The Contagion of Forgiveness / 122

Chapter Seventeen: The Deep Waters of Mercy / 130

Chapter Eighteen: Merciful Nostalgia / 138

Chapter Nineteen: Healing Our Notion of Death / 146

Chapter Twenty: Saint Dismas and the King of Mercy / 153

Conclusion / 160

Notes / 163

Foreword

I have read these theological and spiritual essays with interest and with no small amount of spiritual benefit.

The decision to make Monsignor Magee's writings known is appropriate and timely: They are the fruit of deep and sustained reflection, both theological and spiritual. They are also the fruit of the pastoral solicitude that prompts him to respond to the mental and spiritual anxieties of men and women who seek to give meaning to their lives in these difficult times.

Unfortunately, as Monsignor Magee suggests more than once, the cultural ambience in which we find ourselves has drawn minds and hearts away from the presence and action of God in the world. Some have reached the point of proclaiming the "death of God." Others, who call themselves believers, cut God from their lives, following paths contrary to the law established by God to give light and reason to humanity.

These essays awaken the idea and clarify the fact that, in Christ, the truth that saves has revealed itself. Christ has deposited this truth in the Church to be transmitted by the Magisterium. In the face of the anxiety, doubts and even the desperation of today's men and women in their search for a sure path in life, these writings offer the truth who is Christ, full of mercy toward human misery: the Christ who leads us to the Father by the action of the Holy Spirit; the Christ who has placed his truth in the Magisterium of the Church; the Christ who, in his boundless mercy, wants to save sinful man; the Christ who fills the emptiness and anguish of the human heart.

With enthusiasm and hope, I advise the American public to read this book. In it they will encounter abundant spiritual nourishment, a sure doctrinal guide and a voice of hope leading them to encounter Christ once again and to follow him, he who is the "Way, the Truth and the Life."

—Archbishop Gabriel Montalvo
Apostolic Nuncio
United States of America

Introduction

Each time I go to the barber, I realize I am getting a little older. I also realize, as I look in the mirror, just how much more I look like my dad.

When I examine my conscience, I also see reflected in that interior mirror many of my dad's quirks and much of his goodness. I remember my times of rebellion, and I remember his attempts to discipline me. I remember how often I dismissed him out of hand and how often he would just say nothing. I remember how difficult it could be to talk to him. And when he died, I remember how much I wept. I was so grateful to God for him as the first mirror in which I saw God as my Father, and indeed, myself as a priestly father.

I share this with you because, although in each of us there is a strange need to rebel, deeper down there is also the wonderful need to obey. There is the need to know we have a father who loves us and who, because he loves us, directs us, disciplines us and embraces us.

If someone has not had the grace of such a human father, his or her sense of emptiness, loss and frustration can be fierce. But we all need to remember that, as Christians, the first thing we say we believe in is "God, the Father, the Almighty, the Creator." And the first prayer we learn is "Our Father."

The absence of the love of a human father can surely be a source of great suffering. But do not despair! Rejoice and be confident, for the very absence of a human father throws you all the more fully into the heart of our Father in heaven. Perhaps, for his own kind purposes, he deprived you of the love of an earthly father so that you would depend on and trust more fully in him.

To say God is our Father is not just a way of speaking. It is the fundamental truth, the fundamental hope, the fundamental love of our lives. "Blessed be the God and Father of our Lord Jesus Christ, the Father of mercies and the God of all consolation, who consoles us in all our affliction" (2 Corinthians 1:3-4). These words of Saint Paul ought to be imprinted deep in our hearts, for in any affliction they give life. The Father is as close to us as we are to ourselves, indeed even closer. All we need to do is take time to listen for him, to somehow register his majestic tenderness within us, to let him embrace us, comfort us and lead us along the paths of truth and justice, which he sent his Son to show us.

For indeed, God's mercy is fully revealed in the person and in the deeds of Jesus Christ. If in ancient times the Flood destroyed sinful humanity, in the fullness of time the superabundant grace of Christ destroyed the sin but saved humanity. Jesus personifies the living mercy of God. Even his righteous anger seeks only the repentance of those blinded by sin, that he might show mercy to them.

Repent! Come and follow me! These words of Jesus constitute the entire program of our journey away from the darkness and emptiness of evil toward the light and fullness of the goodness of God.

It is difficult to know if Peter and Andrew, James and John, in the din of their work, heard the voice of Jesus call them at first. What is certain is that that voice was able to penetrate to their hearts. Swept up by the power of his call, they left the entanglement of their nets, left even their livelihood and families, and followed him.

That same voice of Jesus the Lord calls out at every moment to every human being. In the case, for example, of Saints Francis of Assisi, Anthony of the Desert or Ignatius of Loyola, that voice seemed to have a riveting quality that almost violently interrupted the directions of their lives and guided them along the path of holiness.

I too, in my own heart, have heard something of this voice—not in a physical, audible sense but in the silence of the night or of prayer or of suffering. At key moments of my life I have felt the burning fire of excitement and hope that has drawn me out of spiritual sluggishness or fatigue. I have known tears of joy in realizing, in a way that is difficult to describe, that he has come very close to me and clearly called me to repent and to follow him.

"The heart has its own reasons," says Pascal, "which Reason does not know."[1] Somewhere in the heart is the explanation of this deep, personal call of Jesus to each of us.

The angel Gabriel spoke to both Our Lady and Saint Joseph about the coming of Jesus. It was at this deep level of the heart that they welcomed the voice of God's messenger, and it was also at this level that they responded in obedient action.

Christ's voice sweetly yet strongly calls us first to repentance and then to the obedient action of following him. In this way we become imitators of the many saints who have surrendered themselves unconditionally to the divine desire for their love.

No man is an island. No heart is inaccessible to Jesus. Take time, in the quiet silence of the night or any other time, to allow the voice of Jesus to be heard deep within you; listen and act upon his call to repentance and discipleship. For if you do, your inner suffering and doubt will find an end. You will know personally, with indestructible certainty, that God desires you unconditionally, calls you unconditionally, needs you unconditionally and loves you unconditionally. Give your heart a chance to know the greatness of its destiny and the unspeakable greatness of the Lord who so loves you.

It is in this spirit, and to this end, that I humbly offer the following reflections. The twenty essays are edited adaptations of some of the homilies I have had the grace and duty to give in recent years. They present varied approaches to understanding how the Father of mercies reveals himself to us through Jesus in the midst of his Church. I pray fervently for the consolation, peace and joy of all who read them. I also ask for the charity of your prayers.

I want to thank Cynthia Cavnar for her inspirational encouragement in this initiative. Thanks also to James Garcia and Father Gerard Conroy, two of my most treasured and faithful friends. Although there are many others who, in one way or another, have contributed to this work, I want to thank especially the Most Reverend Archbishop Gabriel Montalvo, Apostolic Nuncio to the United States of America and His Eminence Theodore Cardinal McCarrick, archbishop of Washington.

These notes of thanks would be incomplete if I did not mention the patient and generous-hearted priests and parishioners of the Cathedral Parish of St. Matthew's in Washington, D.C. May the Lord's mercy fill their days with joy and zeal for the kingdom.

PART ONE

Mercy and the Trinity

The LORD, the LORD, a God merciful and gracious, slow to anger, and abounding in steadfast love and faithfulness, keeping steadfast love for the thousandth generation, forgiving iniquity and transgression and sin.
(Exodus 34:6-7)

Being and Giving Forgiveness

And forgive us our debts, as we also have forgiven our debtors. (Matthew 6:12)

You wicked slave! I forgave you all that debt because you pleaded with me. Should you not have had mercy on your fellow slave, as I had mercy on you?
(Matthew 18:32-33)

The words from the parable of the wicked servant explain the meaning of the quoted petition of the Our Father. I will try to articulate a few of the many points pregnant in that explanation.

God Is Forgiveness Before He Gives It

Forgiveness is not ours just because we ask for it, as if the initiative were ours alone. Theologically understood, forgiveness does not follow an *ad hoc* question-and-answer session. Forgiveness begins with God. It is the gratuitous and permanent manifestation of God's very own being to the sinner. The essence of forgiveness is not judgment or emotion, morality or psychology. Rather it stems from the very nature of who God is. God *is* forgiving in the depths of his being.

The term *forgiveness* is a conceptual expression of the relationship between God as love and us as sinners. Think of the encounter between the Prodigal Son and his father: The "classical" sinner meets the quintessential forgiver.

Forgiveness always precedes the sinner's petition. Indeed, it is the forgiving God who steals into the spiritual memory and into the conscience of the sinner and sweetly questions if he or she is lacking anything.[1] Forgiveness is not, then, a human idea or initiative; it does not belong to the order of human justice or sentiment. If God is love, God is forgiveness. As the old saying puts it, "to err is human, to forgive is divine."

The divine is not invulnerable. It is precisely our legitimate but limited understanding of God that sometimes leads us to consider him as a monolithic and impregnable block of stone. But omnipotence does not equal impassivity: God is not an iceberg; he is infinitely tender, a consuming fire.

God gets hurt in ways we can only imagine—or never imagine. The hurt caused by our sin so pains God that he employs his omnipotence to eliminate it, without eliminating us. He is hurt because we are hurt; his pain is a pain of compassion.

That is the motive and the meaning of the redemption, of the passion of the Christ: destruction of sin, salvation of the sinner. The Cross of Jesus is where the love of God zealously destroys that which destroys us. In the body of Christ crucified, Love itself and sin itself are ignited in a passionate duel. By the physical death of Christ, forgiveness, the greatest power for good in the universe itself, annihilates sin, the greatest power for evil.

So we must think twice, not to say seventy times seven, before we casually indulge in sin, tolerate sin, do deals with sin or withhold forgiveness from others. What Jesus did for us took place in space and time but is not limited to either. By virtue of his divinity, the value and relevance of the redemption span history and geography. They are present always and everywhere.

Equally, by virtue of his divinity, he draws the sins we commit here and now into his work of redemption, that they might be "never and nowhere"—that is, destroyed. He dies that our trespasses might be forgiven, that we might be made free.

The Duck's Back

As Jesus recounts in the parable of the wicked servant, when the master realizes that the one forgiven does not forgive his brother, that master is angry, hurt, devastated. His generosity, not to mention the cost he willingly sustained, obviously meant nothing to the one forgiven.

It is not God who is to blame for the wicked servant's fate: If the wicked servant accepted forgiveness, that forgiveness would have made him forgiving. In failing to forgive, he lost the forgiveness that had been offered to him. He lost the chance of being made new.

Why do I speak of forgiveness being *"offered* to him"? Because had he truly received that offer and made it his own, made it part of himself, made it wisdom gained from experience, he would not have throttled his neighbor. If in God forgiveness is metaphysical—that is, essential to his nature— then so it must be in us. Before it is a word, a gesture, a concept, an emotion, an attitude or even a virtue, forgiveness is a way of being. As God is forgiving, so am I forgiving. If I have truly embraced with my deepest soul the forgiveness of

God, God communicates to me a share in his own divinity. That is the meaning of sanctifying grace.

Forgiveness does not tear a page from our record book or wipe clean a slate or scrape a pot somewhere in the nether regions of our soul. If to forgive is divine, to be forgiven is to be made divine. And to be made divine means I myself make others divine by forgiving them from the depth of my soul.

Now, the wicked servant treated forgiveness like water off a duck's back. It did not get inside him. He read it as permission to go back and do more of the same. Had he not been called to account, he really would not have accepted the fact that he had done anything wrong in the first place. For him there was no intrinsic evil but only the inconvenience of arbitrary justice. The fact that he would throttle his neighbor and threaten the same punishment he would have received, for something much less than he himself owed, suggests that he saw no difference between his crime and his neighbor's.

To have and to spend were his concerns, irrespective of the damage to himself, his wife, his children and to his neighbor and his neighbor's wife and children. In his arrogant self-concern he did not even realize that others would spot his hypocrisy and appeal to the master against him. He did not understand that being forgiven was the opportunity to be free of his addictive egoism. Being forgiven would create a new heart and spirit within him, enabling him to live in humble peace with his master and in fraternal joy and understanding with his brothers (see Psalm 51:10). His soulless darkness would have become bright as day.

Forgiveness is not a consumer item of the spiritual order: It is the reconstitution of our dignity and freedom as human beings and as children of the Most High. Forgiveness

is our calling in two complementary senses: We are called
to receive the forgiveness of God and of others who have
known his forgiveness; and we are sent to forgive as God has
forgiven us and, indeed, as we have seen in the example of
those others.

Forgiveness is both vocation and mission, indicative
and imperative, grace and cross. With the exception of Christ
himself, only the one who has been forgiven can forgive,
because only the one called can be sent. Only the one who
has received can give. The little word *as* in our petition ("forgive us...as we forgive") tells us the same thing. It is not that
the Father must model his forgiveness on our forgiveness; it
is not that God, like some businessman, is only going to give
us what we pay for. Rather, we can only take in his forgiveness if we ourselves have hearts open to that forgiveness.
And we cannot have hearts open to his forgiveness if we are
unwilling to give the forgiveness we receive to those who
trespass against us.

Like all grace, forgiveness recoils from monopolies: Our
request for forgiveness is sham if we do not receive it in order
to give it. Forgiveness is for giving, not for keeping. If we subject forgiveness to solitary confinement in our hearts, it will
itself imprison us and will not let us out until we have paid
the very last penny.

Mercy Presupposes Truth and Justice
It is clear that, of ourselves, we are unable to forgive; and
even with the help of God it is still not easy. As God distin-
guishes between sin and sinner, we must do the same to
those who offend us.

Forgiveness is not moral blindness. Forgiveness is not "okaying" anything and everything; if that were true, forgiveness would not be needed, for everything would be "okay." Just as God sees and names and eliminates sin, so we must try and see it, say it as it is and bid it forever good-bye.

To forgive genuinely is to sustain the cost of the pain caused by the other, to absorb that pain and to respond to the guilty one with Christlike compassion. This does not mean we should refrain from speaking the truth in love. To forgive is to give new life to a dying relationship. It is to restore hope and joy. It is to see and love the image of God in the other beyond the decoys of sin.

Certainly, if one is willing to forgive but the other is not truly responding, then to remain forgiving involves a real crucifixion. It is, however, to this that we are called and empowered by the sacraments of forgiveness that we receive. Forgiveness may be conditioned because of the one who will not seek nor accept it, but if it is real, the one who is offering it does so unconditionally. Otherwise we are not forgiving as we have been forgiven.

Forgiveness speaks to God's realism about us and to his "mad" love for us. Not only have we all sinned, but we cannot save ourselves from sin, nor can an individual be saved from it if he or she does not want to be saved. We do not need to look further than our own selves to understand this.

Law and order can certainly fight evil in the world, but they can do evil too if they are not exercised according to God's truth about human beings. Law and order are easily hijacked, if not in letter then in spirit. When human law drifts or is driven from the fundamental principles of the natural law, it oppresses under the guise of civil righteousness. Even if we do follow natural law, as we surely should, we might end up in the paradoxical situation of collective pride and arrogance because "we did it ourselves." And in the battle between good and evil, pride surely falls on the side of evil: "Pride and arrogance and the way of evil and perverted speech I hate" (Proverbs 8:13).

Grace can work with sovereign freedom both within and beyond law and order. It is only and ultimately by grace that the human family can labor with effective freedom for lasting justice and peace. It is only that manifestation of grace known as forgiveness that can fully identify and destroy all trespasses and restore nobility and harmony to the human race.

There is no greater hope of peace than heartfelt forgiveness, for there is no greater expression of the power of God among sinners than his omnipotent mercy. We must beseech it for ourselves and shower it abundantly upon one another. Then God and others will forgive us as we forgive. Then we will be able to pray in spirit and in truth to the God who is our Father in heaven.

On Reflection

Imagine you had to describe to a child the difference between true forgiveness and false forgiveness. How would you say it?

If God is all-forgiving through Christ and through the Church, how do you reconcile this with the teaching of Jesus to the apostles about forgiving sins and retaining sins (John 20:23)?

Even after a good and sincere confession, you can still feel attracted to the very sins you just confessed. Why is that?

✠

Merciful Lord, in you mercy and truth have kissed (see Psalm 85:10). Your Cross reconciles your forgiving truth with our sinful truth. Make us willing forgivers in your image and likeness; let us not allow sin and vengeful justice to be the basis of our relationships.

May we confess in truth our iniquities so that we may profess in truth your holiness, manifested most powerfully and most beautifully in the forgiveness of sins. *Kyrie, eleison.*

CHAPTER TWO

The Forlorn Father

The younger son gathered all he had and traveled to a distant country.... [The elder son] became angry and refused to go in. (Luke 15:13, 28)

It is out of the abundance of the heart that the mouth speaks. (Luke 6:45b)

These words Jesus speaks in Luke 6 apply above all to his own heart. The parable of the Prodigal Son, which his mouth speaks, reveals the "stuff" of which the heart of Jesus is made. It tells us above all that he knows the heart of God the Father, and it tells us the story of human sinfulness from the viewpoint of the Father's heart.

Poisoned Relationship

Jesus identifies two types of son and sinner, one more obvious and flamboyant and the other more subtle and routine. Both essentially ignore their greatest treasure, which is simply to be sons of their father. With astonishing ingratitude they focus their hearts on the material things that the father gives them as his beloved sons. They neither understand nor appreciate the heart of their father; rather, they are obsessed with themselves, with their own preferences and good pleasure.

This is all too evident in the younger son and barely masked in the elder. Neither sees the father as father and so no longer understands what it means to be son or, therefore, brother. Their ingratitude has made them orphans; their greed has stolen their dignity and sense of solidarity.

The root sin of the parable is not the departure of the younger as opposed to the staying of the elder. Nor is it the younger son's womanizing as opposed to the elder's desire to socialize with his friends. It is not the younger's waste of money as opposed to the elder's saving it. Nor is it that the elder refused to join the feast while the younger sailed right in. It is not that the elder was angry as opposed to the younger being repentant. It is not the jealousy of the elder as opposed to the trust of the younger.

There are, surely, many faults involved here, and we must see them and call them for what they are. But the root sin is that the hearts of both of them are *closed to the love of their father*. Indeed, we get the impression that they manipulate and use their father in order to get out of him their selfish wants. The father is effectively no longer father but has become an obstacle to their inheritance. What the father has should be theirs!

Being physically close or far from the father is not what constitutes love or lack of love for him. Certainly closeness ought to mean at least a desire to love him, yet the elder's son's attitude is anything but loving. Both the younger and the elder son are driven by the question, "What can I get out of my father?"

When Jesus told the apostles that they must renounce riches for his sake, Peter responded, "Lo, we have left everything and followed you. What then shall we have?" (Matthew 19:27). What a typical expression of human self-seeking! It is the poison of all relationships; it is the poison of original sin, in which Adam and Eve reached out and tried to "get the godhead" for themselves.

Consumerism is as old as the hills and as dangerous as the serpent's bite. Dressed up in seductive words and images and buoyed by the secularist dogma that everything you want is good and no one has a right to stop you, we literally choke ourselves, drown ourselves, exhaust ourselves in our own unbridled appetites. Though legitimate up to a point, the "What about me?" attitude can lead to murderous self-centeredness. We perceive it—masked and unmasked —behind the decaying dimensions of contemporary society, at least in the West.

First Things First

The words of Jesus come to mind: "For what will it profit them if they gain the whole world and forfeit their life?" (Matthew 16:26). It is easy to see that greed is idolatry. In gorging the heart, avarice actually steals our heart from us, just as it steals our ability to recognize or believe in the sincerity of the love of others. In our misery, no matter how happy we may think we are, the heart of the Father suffers and pines for us to reclaim our hearts from the ruin of greed to the salvation of self-surrender to him. For his gifts are given out of love, that we might be drawn to his heart, not that we might ruin our own.

In what the father says to the elder son, "You are always with me, and all that is mine is yours" (Luke 15:31), Jesus is telling us that, as far as the Father is concerned, simply being with him is already to possess everything. We can have nothing greater than God himself. We cannot take our relationship with God for granted nor banish it to some far-off realm we consider irrelevant to our daily lives.

The parable of the Prodigal Son is, among many other things, a call to remember the first commandment: "I am the Lord your God...you shall have no other gods before me" (Exodus 20:2). First things first. If we know God in truth, then we will necessarily love him in truth. In that love our humanity will flourish and blossom.

Failing to keep the first commandment makes observance of the rest nigh impossible.

In taking God for granted, we ignore him, manipulate his gifts, create enmity with one another and eventually fall into the whirlpool of self-destruction. To ignore God, even if we claim to know him or to be near him, is to lose the foundation of our identity. Personal and communal integrity are possible only in direct reference to and dependence upon God.

The fact of the matter is that if God alone is not your Father, your Almighty, then anyone and anything can become your god. You cannot make God merely a factor in the social equation. He is the foundation of all equations.

God is not a useful theory to justify a conservative outlook over a liberal one or vice versa. We cannot invoke him as justification to do what is hateful in his sight. God is not a mascot, a security blanket, a drug, a principle, a big bang or a fascinating concept. God is not a bottomless pit of the kind of mercy we invent for ourselves to legitimize persistence in sin.

God is God. He will not be mocked, and whoever manipulates him does so at his own peril. God's mercy is surely infinite, but if you do not desire that mercy as he reveals it, and on his terms, it will not—for it cannot—rescue you.

Fatherless and Free?

In our parable Jesus portrays the Father as exquisitely respectful of the freedom of his sons. Divine love does not assume the right to impinge upon human freedom. However, when we do freely turn to him, albeit just to find bread to eat, his response of love is unmeasured.

We cannot reasonably be angry with God when he does not do what we would do. After all, who created whom? If God followed our approach to things, Jesus would never have made it possible for us to return to our Father's arms and festive hospitality. Now that return is possible, we cannot say that we want to be free to do what we want and, when things go wrong, blame God for not saving us from our freedom! Either we are free or we are not—and indeed we are! Either God is free or not—and indeed he is!

Sure, his love for us is so great that he comes as near as possible to our inner sanctuary of freedom, hoping to attract us to himself. But he will never violate our sanctuary. He sends us many signs of his love: the order of creation, the truth of his Son, his active providence for each and all. But he will not overwhelm us unless we signal him to do so.

This the younger son did when the father ran to embrace him while he was yet a long way off. Meanwhile the elder son, though still sharing a house with the father, by his own volition remained the more distant from him.

We are all aware, I think, that the drama of the two sons, not to mention the more painful drama of the forlorn father, is still as relevant today as it ever has been. As a civilization, many of those in leadership, and those hoping for it, many of those responsible for forming public opinion and policy, have effectively and efficiently removed even the memory of God the Father from communal life. We are becoming a society of orphans, a fatherless society, a godless society.

Recent trends of thought, such as atheism or agnosticism, are not, I believe, to blame for this. Worrying though they are, they are not as worrying as those who *say* they believe in God but actually exclude him except in appearance and when he does not get in the way of their plans. But if God is who we say he is, can we really separate him from any dimension of human existence, individual or collective?

The autonomy of the secular order is only legitimate when it does not presume itself to be exempt from the judgment of God. Human beings can make even God an object of consumerism: "We want you there, not here! We want you then, not now!" The issue is immensely complex, and the nervousness about it, while understandable and not always unjustified, is considerable. However, these should not prevent us from defending and promoting a worldview that is compatible at least with the first commandment and with the underlying wisdom of the parable of the Prodigal Son. Such a view is monotheistic without being theocratic.

We must articulate this view to modern civilization, with total fidelity to God and convincing reasonableness. For those Christians who, knowingly or unknowingly, have drifted completely away from him—and we are all in danger of that—we must pray that they will remember their Father's house and, as the text says, come to their senses (see Luke 15:17).

We will convince no one to return, however, if we ourselves fail to witness to the mercy of God in the way we deal, dialogue and discuss with others. It is telling that the parable makes no mention of any greeting between the younger and the elder brother. If we are among those who think they are still "at home," anger or smug superiority are the last things we should be showing to those we think are not.

Only Jesus can give us the wisdom and courage of mind and heart to be the pathway by which others can come back to God. His heart, in oneness with the Father and the Holy Spirit, is abundant in meekness and gentleness. May our hearts be one with his, for he is the only life-giving source of what our mouths can speak in witnessing to the merciful supremacy of God the Father.

On Reflection

God as Father and the forgiveness of sins are articles of faith. What does this tell me about the call to give and receive forgiveness?

Do I live my life in the awareness of God as my great and good Father? How can I improve on that?

Do I find that being forgiven, especially in the sacrament of penance, translates into a grace-filled attitude of forgiveness toward myself and others?

What specific area of my life needs to open up to the forgiveness of the Father?

Who is that person whom I refuse to welcome home to my heart? What steps do I need to take to change my attitude?

In what ways am I the younger son, and in what ways am I the elder? In what ways might I even be the father?

✠

Tender and merciful Father, may the memory of your home bring us to our senses when our sins have landed us with the pigs and starved us of the bread of your Word. May we be moved to tears of repentance at the thought of your running to embrace and kiss us. May we be moved to gratitude when your Word celebrates our dignity as redeemed sinners, as sons and daughters at the banquet of your loving heart, our treasure and our home. *Christe, eleison.*

CHAPTER THREE

Spirit-Driven

And the Spirit immediately drove him out into the wilderness. He was in the wilderness forty days, tempted by Satan; and he was with the wild beasts; and the angels waited on him. (Mark 1:12-13)

The Church gives us this text for our meditation on the First Sunday of Lent. To talk of the Holy Spirit on that Sunday may seem a little premature, since in fact we tend to limit our thinking about, and praying to, the Holy Spirit to the times of Pentecost and of the celebration of the sacrament of confirmation. Perhaps we do this because our understanding of the Holy Spirit is somewhat limited or vague.

Yet our faith actually offers us a very rich understanding of the third Person of the Blessed Trinity. At the Last Supper Jesus speaks of him as the Consoler, the Advocate and the witness to the truth of Jesus' own mission in the sight of the Father. Jesus also says at that time that the Spirit will lead the Church to the fullness of truth and, in a more solemn way, that the Spirit will convict, and eventually convince, the world of its sin of unbelief (see John 14–16). Pentecost presents the Spirit as a powerful wind and as tongues of fire. Then there are those series of comforting words scattered throughout the New Testament that capture one or another gift or fruit of the Holy Spirit.

In the Thick of the Battle

The text of Mark cited above highlights something unsuspected, unexpected, strange even, about the Holy Spirit. Jesus is driven, compelled by the Holy Spirit to face the fundamental dilemma of every human being: to choose obedience to what is true and good as God has established and made known, or to choose disobedience to the same and so to surrender to the dominion of Satan.

As true man, Jesus was tempted in every way that we are; equally, as true man and not *only* as true God, he was victorious over every temptation because he freely chose the Father's will. He himself says at one point, "Which of you convicts me of sin?" (John 8:46).

But in Mark's Gospel we see that it is the *Holy Spirit* who *drives Jesus* into the *thick* of the battle, the battle about what is the most profound meaning of being human, of sharing in fallen, ambiguous, mortal, human nature. That strife is precisely the agony of sustaining confident trust in the Father and practical obedience to his will. This reverses the fall of Adam. On the other hand, surrendering to the tendency within us to assert our own perception of what is true and good only adds to the tragedy of the Fall.

We could put it this way: The Spirit drove the first Adam into the Garden of Eden to be tested in his willingness to obey God's ways, but Adam succumbed to the clever, the fascinating, the corrupting suggestions of Satan. Now the Spirit drives Jesus, the new Adam, into the desert for the same purpose. Jesus lets resonate within his human nature not the words of Adam ("It was her fault!") but "Father, let your will be done in me! Let your kingdom come in me!"

This Spirit-driven battle and agony of Jesus will last until he gives up the spirit on the cross. His free and persevering choice of faithful obedience to the Father sows the seed of the new creation, the new Adam, and of the possibility of redemption for the old Adam. It is a seed that eventually blossoms in his resurrection and will flower in its fullness, will attain its highest intensity of aroma, only at the resurrection of all the faithful from the dead.

Here lies the substance of our hope of personal redemption; here lies the pattern of what must be reproduced *in* each of us, if the old Adam or Eve in us is to be renewed and to flourish with redeeming grace. The battle of temptation in the desert of life is, on one side, the work of the Holy Spirit driving us to choose Christ as our strength, our wisdom, our mighty hero (see Jeremiah 20:11), our King, companion and Lord. On the other side of that battle is the connivance between the person of Satan (and Satan does exist!) and our own personal evil, with the aim of rejecting Christ, of killing Christ, of declaring the death of God.

This is the warfare of Lent. It is the warfare that underlies our daily and lifelong struggles to choose what is true and good and beautiful in the sight of God. But unless we engage in this battle, our faith is at best an intellectual prop to justify our ideological preferences; our hope is a naïve and presumptuous optimism to avoid facing the truth about ourselves; our love, however intensely felt and protested, is mere emotion, a faint parody of the last cry of the dying Christ.

Temptation's Transforming Fire
Temptation is not sin. You do not have to confess your temptations! Sin is the free but wrong use of the good things God

has given us: goods of nature and goods of grace. But temptation is the opportunity *we need* to use those gifts aright, according to God.

The right choice in the hour of temptation is to allow the waters of our baptism to well up within us, lifting us from one degree of openness to the kingdom's presence within us, to a higher and more intense degree of the same. Temptation is how God tests us and perfects our trust in him. It lets *us* see what the motivations of our hearts really are. Jesus humbly accepts the same challenge by being driven by the Spirit to encounter Satan and all his works, to do battle with him—and to prevail.

God, then, does not tolerate temptation for temptation's sake. Because of Christ's victory, temptation is the route by which we enter ever more deeply into his mind, his sentiments, his heart, his style, his sufferings and his joy. We receive the grace of the Holy Spirit in different ways—such as in the sacraments and through the Scriptures. This grace establishes and consolidates itself when, with freedom and transparency of intention, we stand up for Christ and stand with him against Satan and his sophisticated but all too boring works of destruction.

Only by passing through the fire of temptation, driven by the Spirit and with our hearts fixed on the face of Christ, will we be able to respond to Christ's call to repentance. For repentance, although made up of small and single acts (which are very important), needs to become more. That *more* is not just a way of thinking, nor even just a lifestyle, but the very core of who we are and what it means to be who we are.

Belief in the Gospel is not simply a catechetical knowledge of its doctrine; no, it is an inner revolution. It is a decision to allow the Spirit to break our heart and to plant deep within us a new heart. When we express that new heart to others, it overflows with the truth and grace of the heart of Christ himself.

So it is the driving Spirit who brings about in us the transformation, the transfiguration, of our whole selves into living images of Jesus. Certainly he prompts us, he inspires us, but he also drives us to accept and follow Christ's call to authentic human and Christian maturity. The kingdom of heaven is not so much an other-worldly place as it is the crowning of our free and persevering response to the work of the Blessed Trinity within us.

The Holy Spirit is the driving force of this work; Jesus is the model and pattern of this work; the Father of mercies is the goal of this work. It is in the Father's heart alone that we will find the fulfillment of the deepest yearnings of our humanity, for it is he himself who placed those yearnings within us. Our yearnings for him are but a spark of his very own yearnings for us, for each one and for all.

So fear not in the hour of temptation! It is also the hour of deliverance, of grace and salvation! Recognize it as a graced opportunity to surrender to the work of God in you: to bring you to repentance, to give you a believing, gospel heart and to bring you home to the heart of God, the only destiny truly worthy of the human being he has created and redeemed by the blood of his beloved Son.

And when you get wounded in the battle, let the Spirit drive you to the sacraments of penance and the Eucharist, that you may be healed. Wounds inflicted by evil are sweet and seductive, but if left untended they fester and poison the soul. The wounds inflicted by God make us face up to the bitter truth of our misery so as to heal us with his abounding mercy, poured out for us in the cup of salvation.

God does not test us beyond our ability, so we can trust him in whatever trials and temptations come our way. This enables us—and not only during Lent—to be companions of Jesus and to let the driving power of his Spirit be our courage and strength. As a result we will be conformed ever more fully to the beautiful and glorious Son of God.

On Reflection

Spiritual escapism can often underlie religious piety. In driving us to face evil in the hour of temptation, from what does the Holy Spirit prevent us escaping?

In the Creed we identify the Holy Spirit as the "Lord and Giver of life." How is he life-giving when he drives us to be tested?

Alertness to the promptings of the Spirit implies also alertness to those of evil. How alert am I, and how alert is my marriage, my family, my parish and my country, to the presence and works of both the Spirit and of the evil one? How can I best prepare myself for temptation?

Why is temptation not sin?

☩

Merciful Jesus, you willingly shared in the thick of humanity's battle against the power of evil. You conquered its works forever by the victory of your Cross. Grant me the Spirit of fortitude and vigilance in the midst of life's trials, that I may trust and know that your grace is enough for me. Turn my heart at all times to your most wonderful Spirit, that I may remain free from sin. For where your Spirit is present, there is true freedom. *Kyrie, eleison.*

CHAPTER FOUR

Remembering the Healer

And as they went, they were made clean. Then one of them, when he saw that he was healed, turned back, praising God with a loud voice. He prostrated himself at Jesus' feet and thanked him. (Luke 17:14c-16)

Remember Jesus Christ, raised from the dead, a descendant of David—that is my gospel. (2 Timothy 2:8)

By the end of Mass how many of us remember what the Gospel reading was? Why, indeed, do we forget so easily? Why do we remember some things without any problem yet forget others almost as soon as they are over?

The memory is a very complex faculty of the soul. In it resides the imprint of things we have seen, heard, touched, tasted, smelled. It can pick out the voice of someone we know from the voices of many others. It recalls facts and data, but it also recalls deep feelings of love and of pain. It associates a color with a past experience of joy or of terror. It attributes to a smell a whole world of relationships and circumstances long since forgotten.

Even more deeply, the memory guarantees our identity, for how can I know who I am from one day to the next if I forget who I was the day before? The memory is our lifeline with the past and also with the future, for I can only be who I want to be tomorrow on the basis of who I am today and who I was yesterday. The memory is the key to coherence and consistency in the meaning of one's life, of one's relationships, of human history itself.

One might even argue that the memory is the stage on which a person knows or chooses anything at all. The memory is where the spirit of a person stores the riches of his or her love and wisdom, as well as hate and folly. A person is as meaningful as his memory (although the amnesiac, of course, conserves human dignity).

Deliberate Forgetfulness?

If memory is so important, why are we so forgetful?

Psychologists tell us that forgetfulness can be a deliberate choice we make in order to exclude from our awareness those things, people and circumstances that cause us pain. The psychologists name this the unconscious. We eject from conscious living all that we perceive as a threat to our sense of security, especially security about the identity we choose to give ourselves.

But in fact the unconscious *cannot* forget, for the unconscious is also part of the memory. I may choose to forget the pain of being an orphan, but that pain remains alive and well in my unconscious. Indeed, the more I seek to forget it, the more it will make itself felt, in anxiety, anger or depression. Repressed memories can destroy a life.

We can confine to the oblivious side of our mind individual persons whose presence would overwhelm the nice little nest we have created for ourselves in life. We can be afraid of love! We can be afraid to be the full stature of the person we are called to be by the love of others, because we prefer some other notion of ourselves. We can shun the greatness of a Francis of Assisi, of a Thomas More, of a Maximilian Kolbe, because we detest self-sacrifice, radical humility, the supremacy of God over politics and the simple joy of being in love with God. We can prefer the self-invented greatness of worldly sophistication, importance and prestige, adding on as a mere *P.S.* that, "by the way," we also believe in God.

We keep the promise of great holiness and God-given strength chained up in the dungeon of our memory because we are afraid it will not fit into the mask we have created for ourselves or allowed others to fashion for us. We deceive ourselves into thinking that we simply cannot be martyrs, virgins, confessors or any other kind of saint. Of course, the "I" who simply cannot be a saint is the puny "I" whom we have invented.

And we are right: Such an "I" cannot be great, for by definition it has confined itself to the mediocre! It lacks openness to the risk of being great, of having strong desires for holiness. It does not want its faintheartedness to be overwhelmed by the valor and courage that come from the bogeyman of Christian challenge.

So we can forget because we want to forget. Rather than face and overcome our fears, we protest that we have none. In so doing, we live only a minimal percentage of the potential of our humanity. Like a mean Scot with a barrel of whisky, we measure out only small drops of ourselves, instead of becoming inebriated and inebriating others by the power for great goodness that lies within. (I bet that's the first time you've read of grace being compared to whisky!)

We live on the edge of ourselves instead of at the heart, and so our love for others is at best lukewarm. Our enthusiasm for great goals and high ideals becomes a frozen and self-defeating form of caution and sham realism, while self-pity replaces self-sacrifice and self-concern replaces self-surrender. Instead of allowing others to feast on the great banquet of who we can be, we begrudgingly offer them crumbs and expect them to be grateful.

The Memory of Memories

When at last we stand before God, the process of judgment will entail his setting before our eyes, with no chance for us to run and hide, everything that we carry in our memory: our sins, our virtues, our fears, our hopes, our joys and our sorrows. He will ask us to accept responsibility for everything that is in us.

Of course, we actually stand before God at every moment of our earthly lives, even when we choose to forget it. Imagine that a person stood before you and could see everything inside your whole being. Your face might smile, but this person could see that your heart was really weeping. How foolish it is to pretend that the Lord is not there as we sin and get lost in ourselves.

Do we believe he is there? And if we do, why do we pretend he is not? Or why pretend that his presence is like that of a dumb and inanimate statue? How can you hide your face from the one who sees into it and not be confounded by your own stupidity?

Nine of the ten lepers were happy to meet Jesus and cry out to him and hear his word of healing. They were glad he was present to them and they to him. Yet they promptly forgot him; they forgot his presence and his word. They became so absorbed in their healing that they forgot the one who healed them.

These lepers did not want the trouble implied in their healing. What was that trouble? The establishing of a relationship with Jesus, the surrender to him of a grateful heart, the acceptance of his will that they rejoice not so much in their physical healing as in a heart now blessed with gratitude for the gift of his self-surrender to them. They did not want him under their skin; they wanted only a skin-deep relationship with him, provided, of course, he cleansed that skin first.

"Remember Jesus Christ!" exclaims Saint Paul (Timothy 2:8). There is an echo of the dying request of the good thief here: "Jesus, remember me when you come into your kingdom!" (Luke 23:42). "Remember me," cried the thief; "Remember me," cries Jesus. "Remember Jesus," cries Saint Paul.

The Church exists for this reason: to be the living memory of Jesus Christ in the world! He is the memory of all memories! The Church is Jesus' own gift to humanity, so that we might never forget him and what he has done for us.

The Eucharist exists that we might "do this in memory of" him. What else does Sunday Mass mean but a response to these words of Jesus? The Church exists to be the memory of Jesus! The church building is itself a sign of our memory of Jesus and of the extremity of his love for the Father and for us.

We keep mementos of our loved ones; the Eucharist, the Church, are our living mementos, not only of one who died but of him who rose again. Surely we want him to remember us when we die, so that we might rise again?

What is all our teaching, our catechism, our sacraments, our hierarchy, our papacy, our theology faculties, our social programs, our capital campaigns, if not one great long and prolonged cry: Remember Jesus Christ, a human being like us, of the line of David, who rose again, destroying the sum of all the enemies of human happiness, namely sin and death?

What is the point of our praying, our rosaries, retreats, Communions, holy hours, confession of sin and of mercy, charitable deeds? What is the point of being married in Christ, being ordained a priest in Christ, being consecrated in Christ, if not that we might remember him with grateful hearts and be signs to remind the world of who he is? He will remember us all on the day of our death and on the day in which human history will have run its course!

Saint Paul was chained in prison so that the memory of Christ might be unleashed among the nations. Why then do we chain away in the unconscious parts of our memories the presence, the power, the liberation, the grace, the glory, the wisdom, of the One whose love for us surpasses all the loves we could ever know in this life? Why do we let our fears and anxieties, our narrow-mindedness, our mundane profanity, our cynicism and skepticism, our vanity and self-concern, take precedence over the blessedness of the memory of our beloved Jesus?

The Unforgettable Memory

Do not forget him, ever, in any place, at any moment, in any circumstance, however painful, however delightful. The very ground of the human heart leaps for joy when it remembers the holy name of Jesus. God gave us a memory for one reason and one reason alone: to remember Jesus Christ. He is the unforgettable memory.

Anything else in our memory must reconcile with Jesus, for he is the sum total and the basic ground of our life: "All things have been created through him and for him...and in him all things hold together" (Colossians 1:16-17). Whatever there may be in you that is not compatible with Jesus will at length be destroyed. If he will not accept it, it simply is not meant to be. Alas, there are many such things in human life.

Pray that Jesus would give you his Holy Spirit, who is the living memory of the living God, that during the time he allots you, you might have the will and the strength to summon from the recesses of your memory everything that is in you. Beseech his light to see, his strength to weep for, any evil or pain. Ask that he let it be redeemed unto him. Beseech his joy that you may rejoice for the good and remain grounded in him.

It is your vocation, your privilege, your duty, to be wholly given over to Jesus. Then you will emerge in the greatness of the holiness that he has destined for you. Then you will truly be who you are. Then you will be unable to forget him, and you will be able to be only the person he has destined you to be. Remember Jesus Christ, and he will remember you when he comes into his kingdom.

On Reflection

What role do I allow my memory to play in my relationship with Jesus? Do I have compartments in my memory, some that Jesus can enter and others marked "entrance prohibited"? Why is that?

What does Jesus remember about me? Why does he remember these things?

As a member of the Church, the living memory of Jesus in the world, how do I remind others of him?

What is the chief way in which the Church remembers Jesus?

☩

Merciful Lord, Jesus, praise to you for remembering us in self-sacrificing love! Praise to you for the Eucharist, given that we might celebrate it in remembrance of you!

Forgive my forgetfulness of your name, your holiness and your love. Forgive my fear of witnessing about you, of stirring the hearts and memories of those around me. Grant me confidence in facing my own memories of pain and suffering, that I might unite them with the remembrance of you in the Eucharist and so find forgiveness and healing. *Christe, eleison.*

CHAPTER FIVE

Questions of the Merciful One

Whom are you looking for?... Whom are you looking for?... Am I not to drink the cup that the Father has given me?... Why do you ask me?... Why do you strike me?... Do you ask this on your own, or did others tell you about me? (John 18:4b, 7, 11b, 21a, 23b, 34)

Good Friday can seem like the Church's official day to get depressed. As we contemplate the man of sorrows before us, all kinds of guilty feelings can surge up within us. We remember our sins, our betrayals, our lukewarm attitudes with regard to the Lord Jesus. Perhaps we could sum up all the negative feelings by simply stating that we feel guilty for being human at all.

And since, according to the calendar, we're not permitted to think yet of the Resurrection or to say the liturgical word that begins with an *a,* we feel bound on that day to grovel in our guilt, to feel satisfaction at the discomfort of fasting and generally to respond somberly to this official day of collective gloom.

If such is our mentality toward Good Friday, we might be making a basic mistake. That mistake is that we are putting ourselves at the center of the picture. The Lord's passion becomes a kind of inverted ego trip that subjects Christ's sufferings to our own. We may even secretly consider that our own sufferings are greater than those of Jesus. We may see ourselves on the cross, not him. We may want to proclaim to the world, "Look how much I have suffered for Jesus and for all of you! Recognize me as today's King of the Jews."

But Good Friday is not centered on our sins, our guilt, our suffering or any such thing. On this day we are called to fast from self-pity and morose introspection. Good Friday is *the* day for having "the same mind be in you that was in Christ Jesus" (Philippians 2:5)—that is, for seeking to enter into what *he* was feeling and suffering, from the moment he stepped into the garden in the Kedron Valley to the moment he was laid in the garden near Golgotha. The Church asks us to shed our own skin and to get under Christ's skin. This shedding is the fruit of ardent petition and God-given grace.

The evangelist John, in his account of the passion, helps us to do this in a particular way. Among other things, he puts no fewer than six questions in the mouth of Jesus. These questions reveal something of Christ's inner soul during his passion—especially if each of us lets them be directed to us personally.

All six questions in turn beckon the listener to question his or her own attitude toward Jesus. They are questions that can reveal a lot of mistaken motives for seeking Jesus. They are questions that force us to examine the truth about ourselves before we presume to say that we know the truth about Jesus.

Whom Are We Looking For?

The first question is repeated, and so it is question one and two. Jesus asks those who come to arrest him: "Whom are you looking for?"

Jesus asks us if we really know whom we are seeking. Are we looking for who he really is, or are we looking for our own image of him? Were we actually to meet him, would we recognize him?

In life we so often look for this or that person who might at last love us unfailingly, who would respond to our yearning for total love. But inasmuch as we look, we find ourselves disappointed because we demand too much. This "too much" is born of unrealistic desire.

In the same way we can look for Jesus to reveal himself to us not as he is but as the person we want him to be. We thus literally idolize him—that is, make him into an idol. In effect we do not know him, and we do not know for whom we are looking.

And so we must ask ourselves: Who is the source of my expectations about Jesus? Is it I, or is it he? Do I expect him to measure up to my desires, or will I let him lift me up to his? In other words: Who is Lord? Is it he, or is it I?

People expected many things of Jesus during his earthly ministry. One can imagine the frustration of Jesus: Why do they demand me to be and to do who and what I am not? Jesus' great pain, and perhaps his greatest, was that he was rejected because he was who he was God ("I AM who I AM," Exodus 3:14). People wanted to eliminate who he really was so that he would conform to whom they wanted him to be.

Here is our great temptation: to tell Jesus who he is and then to look for him thus. In so doing we kill him, we cut his real self off from our field of interests and concerns, and we pursue, albeit with good intentions, a caricature of the Son of God.

Jesus accepts the fact that we reject him. He answers his own question when he says to those who will arrest him: "I am He" (see John 18:5). This causes them to fall to the ground, and so he repeats the answer, "I told you that I am he" (John 18:8). In other words, "I am God." He lets himself be taken for a sinner, be bound and be trailed along from one phony trial to another. He sees our blindness, and by yielding to its furious demands on the cross, he "became the source of eternal salvation for all who obey him" (Hebrews 5:9)— that is, all who accept him as he is.

Whose Cup Must I Drink?

The third question helps us understand who Jesus understood himself to be and asks us if we are able to accept its implications. To Peter, impulsive old Peter, Jesus turns and asks, "Am I not to drink the cup that the Father has given me?" (John 18:11b). Jesus' deepest self-awareness is that he is the Son, living in constant loving dialogue with the Father and sent on the mission of salvation by him.

It is not a closed dialogue or one of no consequence. One might imagine that the central topic of conversation between the Father and the Son is, "How can we win humanity back to us?" The divine way of doing just that is to send the Son to save us. The cup Jesus is given to drink is whatever is necessary to bring about our salvation, no matter what the cost.

Peter tries to interrupt that dialogue and to throw away that cup, because Peter still doesn't know whom he is looking for. He still does not understand that the only sword that will glorify Jesus and save us is the word of the psalmist in the mouth of Jesus: "Here I am.... I delight to do your will" (Psalm 40:7-8).

This third question echoes another Jesus spoke once to James and John: "Are you able to drink the cup that I am about to drink?" (Matthew 20:22b). We wouldn't so much mind Jesus' drinking from the Father's cup if it did not mean that we would have to do the same. This is where our association with Christ's passion, with his obedient relationship to the Father, often becomes academic on our part. We avoid the truth because we want to avoid the suffering it brings.

The truth of our baptism is that it is the baptism with which Jesus was baptized, not only sacramentally but in daily life. When the cohort fell to the ground at Jesus' response to their question, Jesus could have taken the opportunity to run away. Instead he boldly repeated the question, taking, as it were, the stem of the cup in both hands, poising himself to drink it to the dregs.

There are many occasions that challenge us to take a stand for who we really are. So often we either become defensive like Peter or evasive like the young man who ran away naked from Gethsemane. We do these things to the degree that we distance our inmost selves from the "mission dialogue" of Jesus and his Father. Only in the experience of God's love do we find the motivation, the strength and the perseverance to step boldly forward with Jesus. Such an experience can only be ours when we know whom we seek.

Questioning the Unreasonable

Questions four and five find Jesus before the high priest. Both questions reveal Jesus' grief at the suspicion and gratuitous violence with which he is treated. When asked about his teaching, Jesus responds to the high priest: "I have said nothing in secret. Why do you ask me? Ask those who heard what I said to them" (John 18:20-21).

The high priest suspects Jesus of having a hidden agenda, of having a secret doctrine that would be blasphemous and subversive. We see a basic refusal on his part to trust that Jesus is honest. When Jesus says, "Why ask me?" the high priest and the guard get irritated and dispense an unreasonable and gratuitous slap in Jesus' face. This is as if to say, "Don't try to get out of it. Don't pretend there is nothing secret."

The suspicion of the high priest convinces him he is right, and he is none too pleased to hear Jesus say he is wrong. The high priest is perhaps thinking, "Since I suspect there is something hidden here, there must be something hidden." He is blinded by his own arrogance. But Jesus responds to violence with reason in his fifth question: "If I have spoken rightly, why do you strike me?" (John 18:23b).

Have you entertained suspicions about Jesus? Do you wonder if he has really told you everything about himself and his plans? When things don't work out as your holy will desires, do you begin to suspect that Jesus is not so loving after all? When you tell others of some suffering you are undergoing, are you suspecting the Lord of somehow enjoying your suffering?

These are all issues of control: The high priest felt he was losing control or had no control of Jesus with his clever replies, and he compensated for the lack of moral control with a smack of physical control. When we blame God, are we not trying to control him? When his Word challenges us to stay open and hoping and trusting in him, but we get angry and irritated and close the Bible, are we not slapping him in the face?

Do we insist on getting a personal answer from him to our questions and worries when he refers us to the Church, to which he has already said everything? Is this not somehow unreasonable and suspicious?

Question or Opportunity?

In the sixth and last question, Jesus tests to see if Pilate is setting a trap to condemn him or is showing an interest in believing in him. "Pilate…asked him, 'Are you the King of the Jews?' Jesus answered, 'Do you ask this on your own, or did others tell you about me?'" (John 18:33-34). It's almost as if Jesus is hoping that, even at this stage, this pagan man might believe in him. And from the subsequent dialogue between the two and the notes of the evangelist, there is almost a tone of friendship between them. Pilate knows the score; he knows the real reason for the process against Jesus: the jealousy of the Jews. But Pilate's ancient idols of power and success suffocate the beginnings of a deeper relationship with Christ and eventually permit Christ's death.

Do we come to Christ out of personal conviction that he is our King? Or do we come to him with, as it were, one foot still in the praetorium, in the milieu of human respect? Perhaps more deeply: Do we come to Christ to see what we might get out of him? Will we drop him when we fear losing social applause or personal advantage?

Imagine the immense sadness of Jesus in losing this Pilate's love, however initial and obscure. Imagine his sadness in losing the love of Judas. Consider the state of his heart when we ourselves use him as a convenience to escape from reality, the reality of our true selves, and, yes, when weabsurdly escape from the reality of his love for us. Do we ask him about himself of our own accord?

> Whom are you looking for?... Whom are you looking for?...
> Am I not to drink the cup that the Father has given me?... Why
> do you ask me?... Why do you strike me?... Do you ask this
> on your own, or did others tell you about me?

Behind these questions lie the salvific sufferings of the Servant of Yahweh, whose obedience unto death unveiled at once God's invincible love for the sinner and unparalleled hatred of sin. May these questions be our opportunity to give answers of love and self-oblation to Jesus, so that each one of us may come to him with a true and sincere heart.

On Reflection

What are my personal answers to the questions of the suffering Jesus?

What are my questions for the suffering Jesus? What are his answers?

What are my questions for Jesus when I am suffering? What are his answers?

✠

Merciful and suffering Lord, many are the questions we ask of you in our troubled hearts; many of them would not be necessary if we were to answer your questions to us, if we would but believe and trust, just a little, in your merciful care! Help us to understand that it is sin that obscures our clarity of vision and our strength of will and leads to the anguish of questioning uncertainty. Help us to be open tothe true you whom our hearts seek and to leave behind the sorry unreasonableness of our sins. *Kyrie, eleison.*

CHAPTER SIX

Exalt the Cross of Mercy

And I, when I am lifted up from the earth, will draw all people to myself. (John 12:32)

The Church celebrates the Feast of the Exaltation of the Holy Cross on September 14. Why this feast at that time, when we are not in a penitential season?

This feast is linked with the dedication in A.D. 335 of the Basilica of the Resurrection, erected over what was considered to be the tomb of Christ outside Jerusalem. It is therefore one of the most ancient liturgical celebrations of the Lord's Cross.

September 14 is roughly halfway between Easter and Christmas. The feast is thus a timely reminder of the central mystery of the Christian faith. This mystery of the Cross accompanies us as a faithful companion in the daily struggles of our Christian lives, when we may feel less buoyed by the great liturgical seasons of joy.

As the sign *par excellence* of our faith, it is fitting that we should recall the Cross at all times, not just when its feast recurs or during a penitential season. The Cross helps us to remember the price of our salvation and to stir up our hearts in love for Jesus, whose very personal memento it is. Indeed, we celebrate the Cross every time we celebrate the Eucharist. That includes, therefore, Christmas and every other "upbeat" commemoration.

God's Merciful Option

Of course, we exalt the Cross not because of itself but because of him who hung upon it, and more especially because of the reason he hung upon it. We do not adore the Cross but Jesus crucified; we are not idolaters but believers. And why was Jesus crucified? The short and truest answer is, to save us from sin and death. But why would he do that? And why did he have to be crucified for that to happen?

It is good and necessary for us to reflect on these questions, because the humdrum and dust of modern living can render us dull and insensitive, ungrateful and indifferent to the great drama of life and death, of good and evil, of love and sin, which is at the heart of each of our lives whether we like it or not. Our routine, our agendas, our more-or-less comfortable lifestyles, our mundane priorities, our presumptuous attitudes, our preoccupation with our rights and freedoms and many other things can cause the most fundamental truths to be sidelined, if not repressed or forgotten altogether.

Let me begin to answer the questions about Jesus' crucifixion by stating the obvious: We are creatures, not God. The reason for stating the obvious is that we often forget it when it comes to living our life! God created us out of pure love and for pure love's sake.

Love is only love if it is freely given. God created us and gave us free will, for to be free was the condition of being able to love him in truth. However, being free also allows the possibility of saying no to God's love. God gambled when he created us free.

Under the jealous influence of Satan, we did in fact say no to God's love. People throughout the ages have failed to trust God's word, to obey his truth. This disobedience is the essence of original sin, whereby men and women freely catapulted themselves out of God's friendship toward enmity, self-destruction and ultimately death. This latter result is not just physical death but spiritual as well, which we can also call hell or damnation.

This self-condemnation, which God had to ratify in justice, did not mean that *God's options* were exhausted. Since God had created us free, he wanted to find a way of rescuing us from sin and death that would still respect our freedom and yet manifest his immense desire to bring us back, to redeem us, to save us for himself.

And just how did he do that? He did not issue a decree from on high canceling our sins and effectively ignoring our freedom and responsibility. God wished to save us *from the inside*, as it were, by becoming true man. Hence the words of Jesus: "For God so loved the world that he gave his only Son, so that everyone who believes in him may not perish but may have eternal life" (John 3:16). The Father sent his Son in the power of the Spirit to become one of us, born of the Virgin Mary.

Faith was the doorway that framed, at one and the same time, God's grace of salvation and our free response to it. The Son of God became incarnate, one of us, so that we might believe in his enduring love. The Incarnation is so incredibly bold and daring that those of other religions, and even many Christians—perhaps some who read this—cannot believe it. They find it scandalous, too good to be true. The true God walked the earth as true man? Come on! Yet here is the source of real marriage, where the two (the divine and the human) become one without losing their specific identities.

Here is the source of the sacraments, where the external and visible mediate to us the internal and invisible reality of the divine.

Whatever It Costs

Jesus did not manifest his divinity all at once, precisely because he wanted to respect our freedom and not overwhelm us. Rather, he appeals to our minds with the proclamation of his truth, the Gospel, the Good News, the annunciation of God's salvation near at hand for those who will freely believe. He also appeals to our hearts and even to our bodies by performing signs or miracles to excite our faith, to draw us to himself. He appeals to the deep sense of loss and confusion within us by showing mercy, by forgiving sins.

Yet he knows, as we all do, that the stubbornness of pride will keep some from believing in him. Indeed, he has aroused the furious anger and rejection of hardened sinners. He knew in his life on earth that rejection would lead to slander, derision, jealousy and even violence and death. Still, he had to be faithful to the will of the Father and to his own will. He had to prove to us that, no matter what we would do, he would remain faithful. He would offer the possibility of redemption to whomever would willingly receive it.

It is at this point that the Cross comes into view. Christ did not want the Cross for the sake of the Cross; he wanted *whatever it would cost* to win over our hearts to faith, hope and love of him. In the historical period in which he was born, and in the place where he chose to be born according to his own inscrutable plan, that cost would involve rejection by the religious establishment of his own people. Some would deliberately misconstrue his mission as being political and not religious (remember that he died as "King of the Jews").

Further, he would experience the humiliation and ignominy of torture and capital punishment at the hands of the Roman gentiles. In this sense the Cross had to become God's answer to our sin, for that was the price that the circumstances of time and place required.

Jesus knew that the Cross would be his fate, and he transformed it into the very instrument of our salvation. For in being crucified, in surrendering himself freely to death out of loving fidelity to the Father and to us, he fulfilled all the prophecies of the Old Testament and brought Judaism to consummation in the sacrifice of the Cross. He became the innocent Lamb who was slain and whose blood saves us from the angel of death and damnation. He became our new and eternal paschal feast, giving us his body and blood as our food and drink for eternal life. His death opened up for us the passage, the corridor, from the hell of sin to the heaven of grace and love.

Why? Because being without sin, death could not hold him. When death "bit" Jesus, it was itself "bitten" —consumed, killed, destroyed. Likewise, whoever believes in him enters by that very act of faith into the corridor formed by his death. This passageway opens not into hell but into heaven, into intimate reconciliation with the Blessed Trinity.

If we marvel at the thought of the passage God made for Israel through the Red Sea, all the more must we marvel with unfailing gratitude at the passage Jesus makes for us through the waters of sin and death. As God blew the waters apart, Jesus breathes his Spirit into the depths of our being. This is the meaning of our baptism. We died with him, and we entered into that passageway from hell to heaven. In a sacramental way we already have risen and ascended with him to the Father.

Without Apology

And so the Cross, by God's design, became no longer the symbol of curse and death but of blessing and life in Jesus, our great and glorious Redeemer. For Jesus was sent not to curse or condemn but to bless and save the world. His resurrection in the flesh is the pledge of our own bodily resurrection at the end of time, when God himself will decide that indeed "it is finished" (see John 19:30).

Without apology, then, we exalt the Cross of Jesus. We sign ourselves with it and bless our children with it. We venerate it and kiss it. We keep it on our walls, around our necks, in our prayer books, in our cars. We must never let ourselves forget the Cross, for on it hangs the hope of every sinner, however miserable; the comfort of every sick person, however pained; the joy of every holy heart, however tried.

We must exalt the Cross more than ever today in our homes, schools, universities, workplaces and recreational facilities, because the Cross speaks of fidelity unto death. It speaks of the extremity of God's love, which is the love that *we need to sustain our own love*—in marriage, in the family, in the Church, in society. The Cross speaks of persevering patience, unconditional forgiveness, limitless compassion. The Cross calms our worldly frustrations and calls the bluff on our ill-conceived and manifold forms of selfishness. The Cross radiates hope when despair seems inevitable.

The Cross can break the hardest of hearts, overturn the most evil designs, bring tears of joy and relief to the most reluctant convert. Before the Cross we all stand judged: What answer can we have for our sins when we look upon the One we have pierced (see John 19:37)? The only answer comes from him: "Father, forgive them, for they do not know what they are doing" (Luke 23:34). Our only plea can be that of the good thief: "Jesus, remember me when you come into your kingdom" (Luke 23:42).

Hold high the Cross! Exalt it, glory in it, for upon it hangs our life and salvation! Do not to let the serpent's subtle suggestions distract you from the Cross. Do not let dust accumulate on it. No matter how important you are, or think you are; no matter how busy you are, or think you are; no matter how intelligent you are, or think you are: Take a moment every day to venerate the scandal of the crucifix and to thank the Crucified for giving himself, for showing us God with such tenderness, vulnerability and humility.

In the hour of temptation, think of the Cross, hold on to the Cross, exalt the Cross, and Satan will quickly withdraw. And in the hour of suffering and final agony, let yourself gaze physically or mentally upon that Cross, for it will be the shape of your doorway into Paradise.

On Reflection

Do I begin to appreciate what it cost the Son of God personally to communicate divine mercy to me? Do I realize, therefore, the serious nature of my sins, be they venial or mortal?

It may seem difficult to confess our sins, but what is that difficulty in comparison to what it cost Christ to make the confession of our sins possible?

Am I ashamed of the Cross of Jesus? Do I honor it in my life and in my living space?

Do I, how do I, when do I, sign myself with the Cross?

The Cross is the power and wisdom of God. Am I ready and willing to let it empower and instruct me?

✠

Merciful Jesus, exalted from the earth upon the wooden altar of the Cross, draw all that is within me to yourself. Bring merciful order to the chaos and confusion of my inner self by focusing each part of me on you. Grant me integrity, wholeness and holiness through the power and wisdom of the Cross.

May the glory of the Cross draw all peoples of all times into the unity of your body. Mark us all with the sign of faith, the sign of the Cross, in the name of the Father, and of the Son and of the Holy Spirit. Amen. *Christe, eleison.*

PART TWO

Mercy and the Church

Through the ministry of the Church, may God grant you pardon and peace, and I absolve you from all your sins. (Rite of Penance)

CHAPTER SEVEN

Prophet of Mercy

In the fifteenth year of the reign of Emperor Tiberius...the word of God came to John son of Zechariah in the wilderness. He went into all the region around the Jordan, proclaiming a baptism of repentance for the forgiveness of sins. (Luke 3:1a; 2b-3)

Arguably Saint John the Baptist was the first Jesuit. Saint Ignatius of Loyola originally called his order the Company of Jesus, to indicate its true leader. We can say that John was one of them not because he was actually a companion of Jesus but because he was the first man to have a deep-felt sixth sense of the presence of Jesus.

Luke's Gospel tells us that the Baptist leapt for joy in his mother's womb when he recognized the presence of Jesus in Mary's womb (see Luke 1:40-44). After hearing the voice of Mary greeting Elizabeth, the Baptist himself became a voice. It is almost as if he wanted to imitate Mary's role in helping others recognize the approaching presence of Jesus.

John's was not the sweet and intimate voice that we would imagine Mary's to be. Nor was it the voice of the religious functionary, the academic, the diplomat or the politician. It was rather the voice of the prophet: intrepid and indomitable, crying out to break the din of sin: "Prepare the way of the Lord!" (Luke 3:4).

John was not interested in pious platitudes, rational discourse, consensus-building or persuasive rhetoric. The

Baptist knew that there was no time and no need for all of
that. What preoccupied and overwhelmed him was that the
Savior was coming, indeed was here, and the people were not
ready for him.

The only way they could be made ready was urgently to
call them to turn away from all mundane distraction, including false religiosity, and to turn toward the coming Messiah.
That was the meaning of the baptism of repentance that he
administered. It was the "U-turn" away from self-concern and
toward the expectant hope of the Lamb of God, who would
take away the sins of the world.

Trumpet Blasts
John was aware of the imminence of Jesus' appearing. So in
his teaching there is little of the explanation that human
beings like before giving or withholding their consent to the
call to virtue. John did not weave long-winded and intricate
patterns of moral reasoning to convince his listeners. Rather,
like a trumpet or a clarion, he blasted forth moral absolutes
to awaken all from their mediocrity: Get yourselves up and
awake and ready to stand beside the standard, the colors of
Jesus your King!

John didn't write a diplomatic letter to King Herod asking for an appointment to talk about his adultery. No, to the
great, albeit perverse, delight of many, he simply denounced
Herod in blunt and public terms for failing to obey the command of God.

With the Baptist there was no messing, no ambiguity or
double-talk, no political correctness or etiquette. He was rude
and crude, direct, unabashed, certain of his message, clear in
its delivery. And he would not take no for an answer. He had

no trouble threatening and applying excommunication, for he knew that when the time is short, people need short shrift in order to be brought to their senses. You can't keep invoking God and defying his law to his face.

There was something apocalyptic about John the Baptist: He knew he was the last prophet of the Old Testament and that the New would bring the fire of judgment. Jesus calls him the greatest of all men born of women and "A prophet, yes...and more than a prophet" (Luke 7:26). The impact of John's ministry upon the Jews and beyond was unequalled since the times of Elijah. It facilitated the beginning of the public ministry of Jesus himself.

Baruch's vision of the restoration of Israel and Jerusalem (see Baruch 5) was full of joy and hope. We hear nothing of that in John, not because Baruch's words were not to be fulfilled but because the people John saw before him were living in a way that was unworthy of that hope and joy. How could John speak of hope and joy when the corruption and moral decadence of his time cried out for the judgment of God?

Woe to the prophet who prophesies peace, joy and tranquility when the society before him has become dissolute (see Isaiah 9:13-15; Jeremiah 5:31; 14:13-15)! How can there be peace when justice is denied, manipulated or emptied of its fundamental meaning? How can there be joy when love has been reduced to comfort, pleasure and mutual admiration? How can there be holiness when evil is exalted as worthy of emulation and good is declared discriminatory, hypocritical or obsolete?

If the prophet were to speak comforting clichés to such a society, he would be only a tool of the self-flattery of fools;

instead of calling them to life, he would be shepherding them on to death. And when judgment comes, the prophet will be asked by the fool, "Why did you fail to point out the error of my ways?" The prophet who goes with the flow will perish with the foolish.

The Merciful Gift of Prophecy

To prepare God's people and all people of goodwill for their encounter with the Messiah, he sends the prophet to speak the truth urgently. God knows how we are inclined to forget the day of his coming. He knows we are anxious and anguished, for he knows the weakness of our wills and the fickleness of our hearts. As a gift of mercy he therefore sends prophets. They will call people to repentance and strengthen their hearts with the clear, penetrating and uncompromising proclamation of the saving truth. They will prepare people for the Lord's coming!

The prophet's job can make him unpopular. Rejection and discord are signs of his success in stirring cold hearts to realize their condition, for that realization at first can bring anger.

Certainly kindness and mercy must be his, but he must take care that neither he nor his hearers get lost in the pleasant landscape of that kindness. He has to spell out the truth. The prophet will reflect the uncanny combination, found in Jesus himself, of warm, charismatic openness and unbending fidelity to the rock of truth. The prophet is both warm and hard: warm in love and hard in steadfastness.

Those who are truly open to repentance will be attracted by that very combination, as were the crowds who went to John for baptism and the even larger multitudes who went to Jesus for healing and hope. Those who are not truly open to the truth will seek to enter the prophet's heart by astuteness, in order to get him to shift his ground. But the true prophet will detect their tactics. The obstinate, by their own doing, will find their fragile lives fractured when they hurt themselves against the rock of truth.

There is something apocalyptic about our time, not because the world is about to end, as far as we can tell, but because important sectors in our human family have become estranged from Christ. The signs are not difficult to read, and they are serious. Whereas in the past the judgment upon generations might have been easier because they did not know God, today people are consciously and deliberately excluding God from their reasoning and decision-making in matters affecting the very structure of the human being, of marriage and sexuality—impacting the survival of the human family itself—and even of the meaning of suffering and death. These dimensions of human life only exist at all because the hand of God has directly given them to us and sustained them. Yet people tell God that he has nothing to do with them.

I have deliberately used the word *God* and not *Christ Jesus* because these matters affect not only the Christian world but also other religions, even theistic bodies that are not strictly religions. Yet it is particularly bitter to note that countries and even continents once proud of their Christian heritage, a heritage that in many cases gave them the very possibility to exist and develop as societies, now wish to exclude Christ.

Think of the recent attempt to remove God from the oath of allegiance in the United States. Think especially of the poor defense of Europe's Christian heritage in the drafting of a European Constitution by the elected leaders of the European Union. It is difficult to understand what people hope to gain by alienating God. As the prophet says, "...They sow the wind, and they shall reap the whirlwind" (Hosea 8:7a).

A New Baptist?

We need the crying voice of John the Baptist today. We hope that God in his providence may send us a new prophet with the Baptist's spirit and uncomplicated oratory, to turn the hearts of children back to their fathers and of fathers back to their children (see Luke 1:17).

Every one of us needs the grace of the Baptist: that deep-felt sense of the presence of Jesus and the fearlessness of spirit to make his presence felt. Discernment and prophecy are not the monopoly of the few; we all receive them in baptism. We may not ourselves be God's prophets for today, but we can help do the groundwork for the ones God sees fit to send. By courageous witness to Christ, through an ever stronger fidelity to our Christian commitment, we can help turn this world, run morally and spiritually amuck, back to God.

The urgent state of the world challenges us to divest ourselves of our complacency and, in deafening chorus with the Baptist, to cry out in our contemporary desert: Repent! Prepare ye the way of the Lord!

On Reflection

It is an article of faith that the Holy Spirit spoke through the prophets, and prophecy continues in the teaching authority of the Church. What is my attitude toward the Magisterium of the Church—that is, to the Spirit speaking through the pope and the bishops to her members and to the world? Consider:

❖ Is my basic attitude one of mistrust and suspicion of motives?

❖ Do I give greater credence to the opinions of science and personal knowledge than to the guidance of the Magisterium?

❖ Is my resistance to the Magisterium more an unwillingness to accept sin for what it is than an intellectually honest critique?

❖ Do I prefer being modern to being obedient?

Why do many people doubt that the Spirit of Christ teaches in his most definitive way through the prophetic ministry of the Magisterium? What can be done to remedy this?

Do I ask the Lord to send prophets in our times to exercise the merciful ministry of calling moderns back from their erring ways?

✠

Merciful Jesus, hear the prayers of Saint John the Baptist for our Holy Father and the college of bishops. Grant them courage, clarity and true charity in the merciful mission of prophecy. Let them neither fear the opposition of men nor doubt the comfort of your strength. Free them from all worldly concerns, that they may proclaim your judgment upon our times with purity of heart and integrity of mind.

May the sons and daughters of the Church, and all men and women of goodwill, rejoice and give thanks to you for the truth your prophets proclaim in your name. *Kyrie, eleison.*

CHAPTER EIGHT

The Cleansed Temple of Mercy

Making a whip of cords, he drove all of them out of the temple... "Take these things out of here! Stop making my Father's house a marketplace!" (John 2:15a; 16)

Cecil B. DeMille's *The Ten Commandments,* with Charlton Heston as Moses, is unforgettable for more than one reason. As a seven-year-old child I was especially struck by the radiance on Moses' face as he came down from the mountain with the Ten Commandments. He had been with God, face-to-face for forty days and nights.

Many years later I came to understand that Moses received very much more than the Ten Commandments when he was up on that mountain. He received some kind of vision or understanding of God's own dwelling place, not on the mountain but in heaven itself. God even told Moses that, "according to the plan for it that you were shown on the mountain" (Exodus 26:30), he was to erect an elaborate tent for Yahweh that Israel would carry on its journey to the Promised Land. Once Israel was settled in the Promised Land, that moveable tent became the immoveable temple, built by King Solomon according to the same pattern.

Other celebrities of the film industry have given us various ideas of that temple. Franco Zeffirelli, in his film *Jesus of Nazareth,* shows Jesus himself standing in awe as a little boy before the temple. This was not Solomon's temple but the one rebuilt after the Babylonian exile. Zeffirelli's film also portrays Jesus' dramatic cleansing of the temple.

The Living Temple of the Incarnation

After they had sinned, Adam and Eve could no longer walk with God or remain in his dwelling. Sin brought, and still brings, exile from God. But God desires to be with us, to bring us back home. From the beginning of Scripture, right up to God's dwelling with humans in the flesh of Jesus, we see God's merciful steps to be with us, to dwell among us.

The patriarchs and prophets knew of God's closeness in many different ways. First he appears in visions to Abraham. He comes to Moses in the burning bush, then face-to-face on the mountain and in the meeting tent (see Exodus 3:2; 19–34; 40:34). To the people he appears as fire on the mountain and as a pillar of fire by night and of cloud by day (see Exodus 13:21). A cloud signals his presence in the tent of meeting. He speaks to Elijah in a small, still voice (see 1 Kings 19:11-13) but later this same Elijah returns to God in a chariot of fire (see 2 Kings 2:11). Isaiah and Ezekiel speak of his "glory filling the temple" (see Isaiah 6:1-4; Ezekiel 43:5).

At last he came not in something made by human hands, nor as a symbolic force of nature, nor in sporadic visions or voices. He came of the Spirit and of Mary, as the Word made flesh who dwelt among us. He came as the incarnate Son of God, Jesus of Nazareth. In Jesus, God's approach to us comes to its full crescendo. In Jesus, all the previous messages, visions, prophecies, laws and covenants come together and are wonderfully surpassed. And the heart of the meaning of Jesus' life and ministry was precisely to bring the exiled home to God's dwelling place, which he achieved by his death, resurrection and ascension.

Given, then, the profound meaning of the Incarnation, it is no wonder that Jesus takes a whip to those who would desecrate the temple. For the temple is now none other than Jesus himself, and in him no sin, no uncleanness exists. To make of the temple a marketplace was to make a marketplace of the incarnate Son: to treat him as an opportunity for gain, as did Judas Iscariot.

The temple was a "house of prayer for all peoples" (see Isaiah 56:7), just as the tent of meeting had been. There Moses had met God face-to-face and interceded for Israel. But prayer is not a negotiation process; it's not a business. To converse with God is not to do commerce with him. For God in Jesus is liberal in his mercy. He asks only that we admit and reject sin so as to embrace that mercy honestly.

Many, but certainly not all, in the religious establishment of Jesus' time had turned Jewish institutional religion into a means to serve their own avarice and their own hunger for power. The attitude of institutionalized self-service had hardened hearts against Jesus. The rejection of Jesus and the self-destructiveness of hearts were symbolized in the Roman destruction of the temple in A.D. 70, which Jesus himself foretold.

But the destruction of the temple of Jesus' body in death was reversed by his resurrection after three days. This victory over death was the sign that gave him the authority to cleanse the temple and, more truly, to determine and cleanse all sin.

The Living Temple: The Church

Jesus had to return to the Father. How then are we to under-stand God's presence among us after the Ascension?

Saint Paul tells us: "Do you not know that your body is a temple of the Holy Spirit within you?" (1 Corinthians 6:19). God's presence with us in the flesh of Jesus remains, but it has now become his presence in the Holy Spirit, poured out at Pentecost on the flesh of all who have believed in him. The visible presence of Jesus has passed into the Church and the sacraments.

In other words, by the will of the Father and the work of the Holy Spirit, we ourselves have been dedicated or con-secrated as the living, Mystical Body of Jesus, as the Church united by the Spirit to Christ our Head. We have become God's dwelling place on earth. The Church is now the tent of meeting, the pillar of fire, the temple of the living God. We are the light on the lampstand, the city on the hilltop, the place where all can and must find welcome.

We not only symbolize the unity of the human family, but we are the "sacrament" of that unity—the outward sign instituted by Christ to give grace. By the Spirit's doing, the Church eventually will effect the unity of the human race through the proclamation of the gospel of Christ in all its full-ness and through the sanctifying ministry of the sacraments Christ gave us.

Some time ago I read in a brief news report that, although the effects of the recent pedophile scandal in the Catholic Church were gradually being overcome, a respectable poll had indicated that Catholics were still reluc-tant to give to the Church as much money as they did before. I wondered whether, beyond the face value of this statement

—which is surely very understandable—the author felt that if no Catholic gave the Church any money, then the Church would fold. Would it be cast into the dustbin of history as yet another failed attempt by human beings to dominate their fellows?

Other polls tell us that Catholics disagree with the Church on numerous moral issues. Curiously, the only issue of divine faith on which there appears to be disagreement is the admission of women to holy orders. So I ask: Will the Church fail even when Catholics fail to believe her teachings?

Will she fail because the lack of money means the closure of schools and hospitals and parish buildings? Will she fail because some of her priests commit heinous crimes or because some of her bishops fail to deal with those priests? Will she fail because of the unhelpful absorption into her members of ideological polarizations, of the desire of some to dominate or exclude others, of pressure from various interest groups or of the mundane preoccupation for career or self-advancement in the ranks of the hierarchy?

The Indestructible Temple of Mercy and Truth

My brothers and sisters, she will not fail, not now, not ever. And the simple reason is because the Catholic Church does not belong to us failing, weak human beings. She belongs to Christ, and Christ will neither fail her nor allow her to fail in the essential mission for which he called her, sanctified her and sent her.

To the degree that we sin, we do indeed loosen or weaken our bond with the Church, and we deprive her of that extra possibility she would otherwise have had to let the light of Christ shine. Yet while our sins may cloud her face and limit her activity, Christ Jesus continues to shine within her, and his Spirit, despite our sins, will at last achieve the purposes of the heart of God for her. The Church herself teaches that she is at one and the same time holy and sinful: sinful because of her members, holy because of her Founder. Holiness shall prevail in her, for the effect of her Founder, the Lord Almighty, the Holy One, is greater than that of her weak members.

The heart of the Church is the merciful heart of Christ. If the Church is the universal sacrament of salvation, she is clearly so as the ambassador of reconciliation, of the merciful gathering of the children of God under her wings. The means of salvation—or mercy and forgiveness—are found in their fullness in her. Already on earth she is the home of the wandering sheep; in eternity she will be the dwelling place of the saints and of the Holy One himself.

The medicine of mercy can only be effective for those who recognize the sickness of their sins; a proud and stubborn heart can ask only falsely for mercy. The sinner must accept the diagnosis of his or her sickness and seek treatment for it. That diagnosis comes from the preaching of the truth of the gospel *as it is taught and understood by the teaching authority of the Church.*

In the end the proud and stubborn cannot ever truly belong to the Church, because the Church, in her final state, cannot shelter anything that is evil. As the dwelling place of the Trinity, she must be spotless, wholly beautiful. Truth and mercy go hand in hand. Refusal to accept the truth is refusal to accept mercy, and no amount of complaining can change that.

As the Holy One, Christ continues to cleanse his temple of sin. One can understand why he might want to take a whip to the Church today, as in probably every generation of her history. Yet each of us who blames someone else for failing the Church ought to ask himself whether that condemning attitude is not itself subject to the first crack of the whip. Blaming is easy and wastes a great deal of time and energy. The mind of Jesus and, therefore, of the Church is surely that we dedicate that time and energy to mutual understanding, forgiveness and reconciliation.

We need the wisdom of the gospel in order to spot the wiles of Satan, who gleefully rubs his hands when Catholics end up in enmity with each other. We need to speak the truth in love to one another. We need together to chasten and chase Satan and sin out of our midst.

We need to block the evil one's attempts to import into the Church the various polarizations that we see in social and political forums. These horizontal antitheses give glory not to God but to egos, groups and parties. They desecrate the Church with manipulations of the truth that suit self-concerned preferences that are alien to the mind of Christ.

Jesus gives us rather a vertical ladder, to pass step by step from sin to holiness, from error to truth, from exile to God. Christ calls us upward, together. We need to let him dedicate and rededicate us to the mind of his Church through prayerful listening to his truth and compassionate understanding of one another from the vantage point of that truth. Rather than buying and selling our own opinions, let us receive gratuitously and with obedient hearts what Christ bestows upon us as the pearl of great price.

It is true that we must be aware of what society says about the Church, but we must process that awareness according to the Church's mind. Why would we listen more willingly to what television, polls, scientists or even eloquent dissidents tell us about the Church? Why not listen with faith and love to the Church herself and to the Lord who speaks to us through her?

Let there be criticism in the Church and calls for accountability, but let these be loyal and motivated by love. And if we so criticize and call, let us be willing ourselves to be criticized and held accountable, trusting ourselves ultimately to the authority Christ gave the Church for the peace and salvation of the world.

When all is said and done, the Church is the treasure of the Christian age. In her resides the hope of all ages. No money can ever buy her, and no greed can ever sell her, for she was bought, cleansed and paid for by the precious blood of Christ. And his precious body she shall forever remain.

On Reflection

What is my understanding of the Church?

How do I reconcile the institutional and administrative sides of her with her deeper mystical and charismatic ones?

When I blame "the Church," who or what am I really blaming? Is there hypocrisy in my blaming?

What is my understanding of my own body? Is it a problem, a tool to be used, a temple to be cleansed and kept clean, a gift to be given in truth to others and to Christ?

What are the implications of baptism for my bodily life?

What can it mean to be merciful in and to the body?

☩

Merciful Jesus, I would rather experience your cleansing anger than treat my own body as a marketplace. Rather still would I experience the deep, cleansing waters of your mercy!

You have given me all that I am and have. Empower me to surrender my whole self to you in your holy Church. Cleanse me from my profanities; let the waters of baptism spring up inside me once again, that others may quench their thirst from the purity of heart and the merciful charity that will flow from within me. *Christe, eleison.*

CHAPTER NINE

Mercifully Catholic

He has made known to us the mystery of his will...to gather up all things in him, things in heaven and things on earth. (Ephesians 1:9-10)

So they went out and proclaimed that all should repent. They cast out many demons, and anointed with oil many who were sick and cured them. (Mark 6:12-13)

Being Catholic can be understood in a number of ways. In some circles the term can be an insult. If you are a sociologist, "Catholic" is just a label for a certain sector of society. Anglicans and Episcopalians often describe themselves as Catholics, meaning that they too hold to the tradition of the apostles, even if we Roman Catholics believe that they do not do so fully. Most Catholics think the word simply means "universal" in a geographical or quantitative sense —worldwide, if you will.

However, the fullest and most proper meaning of the word *Catholic,* from the earliest times of Christianity, was something much deeper; indeed, it was overwhelmingly wonderful. Saint Augustine, for example, instead of using the word *Church* to describe the community of believers, used the word *Catholic* as a noun. The Church was "The Catholic."

In its Greek etymological roots, *catholic* means "according to the whole." It means fullness, completeness, plenitude—primarily of the truth of Christ and of the means of salvation. This was the word the early Fathers of the Church found most fitting to describe, indeed to define, the Church. For them the Church was not just the community of believers but the deep spiritual communion among all believers. Through Jesus Christ this communion extended to the universe itself and, supremely, to the Triune God.

Satan and Sin Poison Catholicism

So *Catholic* is literally, in what appears to be modern jargon, a holistic term. It is the word that symbolizes and sums up the entirety of God's loving mercy for us: in creating us, redeeming us and gathering us together in the body and in the heart of Jesus Christ. The fullness of the Church is nothing other than the fullness of Christ, a fullness he poured out upon us through his death and resurrection and through the sending of the Holy Spirit. On the day of Pentecost the one, holy, Catholic and apostolic Church already existed, and its expanse to the ends of the earth is like the body of Christ himself expanding to embrace the earth and indeed the entire cosmos.

This is something of the meaning of Saint Paul's words quoted above. The apostle expresses with intense beauty his ecstatic and mystical grasp of Christ as the source, mainstay and goal of all creation. When we commune with Christ, in prayer or in the sacraments, especially in the Eucharist, we ourselves become ever more Catholic, ever more complete and fulfilled, ever more plunged into the depths of that mystery that holds the entire universe in existence.

But of course, we often feel removed from this wonderful reality. Our experience of life, both personal and interpersonal, is plagued by brokenness, contradiction, misunderstanding, paradox and sometimes just sheer absurdity. The Christian Gospel identifies the source of this fragmentation in sin, which is precisely our individual and collective rupture of communion with God and with one another.

That sin, however, found its model in the sin of Satan, whose jealousy of humans introduced death into the world. Satan's work is to replace truth with lies, love and freedom with hatred and slavery, and life with death. And indeed, all of us who sin but refuse to admit our sin end up, to a greater or lesser degree, doing Satan's work also.

Satan destroys the intellect and its thirst for truth by feeding it with half-truths and gradually with untruths. He destroys the will and its thirst to choose freely to live the truth in love by feeding it with false loves and false notions of freedom. He destroys the body and its deep-seated yearning for eternal life by feeding it with experiences of self-indulgence, which, under the appearances of physical prowess and happiness, alienate the body from the spirit and render it fit only for eternal death.

Christ and Grace Heal Catholicism

Is it any wonder, then, that the Lord who created us and loved us, and who knows very well the ploys of the evil one, does three principal things in his public ministry?

❖ He preaches the truth of the gospel of repentance to heal our minds.

❖ He drives out evil spirits to restore our freedom for good.

❖ He lays hands on the sick to restore them to health, and even upon the dead to restore them to life.

And what he himself did, he gave power and authority to his apostles to do: "They went out and proclaimed that all should repent. They cast out many demons, and anointed with oil many who were sick and cured them" (Mark 6:12-13).

In the depths of Christ's compassionate mercy for us, as the Divine Physician, he provides what is necessary for us to pass from brokenness, fragmentation and alienation to wholeness, to holiness, to being once again fully Catholic. Now, you may object that, if this were so, why then are we still subject to error, hatred and disease, not to mention death?

The only answer is that, according to God's own plan and wisdom, the fullness of time has not yet come for final judgment and for all things to be restored in Christ. What he desires of us now is that we partake of the struggle, of the agony that was his as he laid down his life for our salvation.

Assailed by evil in subtle and diabolical fashion, Jesus remained focused on his Father's will. Was he not tempted in his intellect to doubt and even reject the truth of his mission? Of course, yet look at the fullness of truth that graciously fell from his lips.

Was anyone tempted more than Jesus to rebel against the will of the Father? No, yet look at the glorious freedom and boundless love he showed to all, *precisely because he remained obedient to the Father*. Obedience is not the enemy of true freedom. The real enemy is disobedience in the name of some self-proclaimed or diabolically insinuated alternative to the truth of Christ.

Did anyone suffer physically and mentally more than Jesus? Most probably not, and yet the chaste, poor and obedient Lamb of God, once sacrificed, now stands at the right hand of God pleading for us.

And his pleading is

❖ that we remain in communion with him through his body, the Church, "The Catholic"

❖ that we open our minds with sincere, devout and religious adhesion to the truth that his apostles teach us in his name

❖ that we open our wills and embrace with freedom and love God's plan for each of us as it unravels in the circumstances of our lives

❖ that we unite our physical sufferings and other sufferings, of whatever nature, to his suffering for us, in order that we may one day hear his beautiful and powerful voice command us, as it once did Lazarus, "My friend, come forth from that tomb!" (see John 11:43).

Christ bore our errors, our rebellions, our infirmities and our death. He destroyed them all. His call is to life, for life, for eternal life!

Catholicism, the Destiny of the Free

Being Catholic therefore means engaging ourselves courageously, in mind, will and body, in the work of Christ. This work is to unite all things in Christ and so bring everything to the fullness for which it was created.

As I said earlier, in daily circumstances it is not easy to keep this grand vision before one's eyes. But that's precisely why we need to proclaim it and re-proclaim it, to pray, to read, to be faithful to the sacraments we have received, to encourage one another in times of distress and to help one another perform generous deeds of charity and holiness. The mass media and our decaying Western culture make it all too easy for the subtle machinations of the evil one, and the evil already in us, to overcome our resolve. We cannot win alone. We need to do it together, united in the Catholic Church. There Christ, notwithstanding all our foibles, remains active and faithful to his promise that the gates of hell will not prevail (see Matthew 16:18).

Sinful times call for *courageous witnesses to holiness*. The human mind can draw many subtle distinctions to avoid accepting the gospel of repentance; we see these all around us. But *we* must remain faithful to "the truth, the whole truth and nothing but the truth" *as Christ feeds it to us through his Church*.

The many perceptions of freedom detached from that truth, and even from truth about our own human nature, make it all the more urgent that *we* understand true freedom as the loving acceptance of the will of God. The prevalence of narcissism in its many forms, which exalts the human body at the expense of its real beauty and meaning, makes it all the more urgent that *we* cherish our bodies as God's first gift to us, that we take care of our health, that we live soberly and chastely according to our state in life.

I end by recalling another truth of the Catholic faith: devotion to the three archangels, Michael, Raphael and Gabriel. God sends these angels to serve us and help us on the road to salvation. For the healing of our minds we can pray to Gabriel, the archangel who announced to Mary the will of God for her: to accept in her womb, for our repentance and salvation, Jesus, the very Truth and Word of God. For the healing of our wills and the casting away of rebellion and false freedom, we can invoke Saint Michael, the archenemy of Satan and victor over him by the power of God. For the healing of our bodies, we can invoke Saint Raphael, God's healing agent, as portrayed in the Book of Tobit.

"Catholic" is not some social tag branded on us on the day of our baptism. It is the program and destiny of our life, here and in eternity. Let us never forget it, lest we forget the love, the sufferings and the glory of our Savior and forget and lose ourselves.

On Reflection

In baptism we became Catholics. We have a fundamental identity as such, but what does it mean for someone to be Catholic in the fullest sense?

Am I proud to be a Catholic, to be known as one and to speak up as one?

What level of knowledge do I really have of Catholicism? *Catholic* means "whole," with a *w,* but where are there holes, with an *h,* in my Catholic life? Do I have a truly Catholic mind, heart and body?

Do I regard Catholicism merely as a social group, or do I show genuine Catholic concern for all the problems of humanity?

Is there a difference between Catholic and Christian? Which of the two terms is truer to the will of Christ?

✠

Merciful Lord, I give you thanks for the Catholic fullness of your gifts to us, a reflection of the unity and of the riches of the life of the Trinity. I am neither whole nor holy because of my sin. Through the merciful abundance of your Catholic Church, heal and reunite the fragmented lives of all people, that in her they may see and experience the sacrament of the unity of the whole human race. Grant me a Catholic heart and mindset, that, always and everywhere and to everyone, I may witness with joy and without fear to your gospel in your Catholic Church. *Kyrie, eleison.*

PART THREE

Mercy and the Sacraments

It will be shed for you and for all, so that sins may be forgiven. (Words of consecration, Rite of the Mass)

CHAPTER TEN

Be Opened!

Then he returned from the region of Tyre, and went by way of Sidon towards the Sea of Galilee, in the region of the Decapolis. They brought to him a deaf man who had an impediment in his speech.... Then looking up to heaven, he sighed and said to him, "Ephphatha," that is, "Be opened." And immediately his ears were opened, his tongue was released.... They were astounded beyond measure. (Mark 7:31-32a, 34-35a, 37a)

The deaf man with impeded speech did not choose to be born that way. Indeed, the characteristics with which we are born are not chosen but rather given to us. This is also true of many of the wounds and hurts that we sustain in life. They are often gratuitous, simply not our fault.

Jesus Groans

Strange though it seems, the healing of those very wounds can be equally gratuitous, even fortuitous. Had Jesus not gone to the Decapolis region, the man in question would most probably have died deaf and dumb. What made the difference?

Both the deaf man and those who brought him to Jesus were sufficiently aware of, and distressed by, his condition. They were also sufficiently alert to the visitation of Providence in Jesus. And so the man's friends became instrumental in turning a tragic situation into one of astonishment—that is, of astounding joy.

Jesus shares in the company's distress; he groans or sighs at the man's pain as he heals him. It is almost as if he were himself absorbing the speech impediment. Jesus also shares, ever so quietly, in the people's joyful astonishment—not so much the psychological and human joy of the healing (though probably that too) as in their spiritual joy at coming to believe in him as Healer, as Savior. It is the joy of salvation of which Isaiah sings with poetic and prophetic beauty, a text the Church relates to Jesus the Healer:

> Then the eyes of the blind shall be opened,
> and the ears of the deaf unstopped;
> then the lame shall leap like a deer,
> and the tongue of the speechless sing for joy.
> —Isaiah 35:5-6

In healing the deaf and dumb man, Jesus performs a little ritual that may seem distasteful to us today. He puts his fingers in the man's ears and saliva on his tongue. It was commonplace in those times for healers to impart their healing power by touching the afflicted areas. Saliva was considered a life-giving element.

But more important than any ritual is the prayer of Jesus. He groans to the Father as he looks heavenward and says: "Ephphatha… Be opened!"

Perhaps some of you will recall that, during the rite of baptism, the priest or other minister performs a version of that same rite. He blesses the ears and lips of the baby or adult, adding the prayer that the newly baptized might always have open ears to hear the Word of God and a loosened tongue to proclaim it plainly. What is now sought is the healing not of the physical faculties of the baptized but of the spiritual faculties of listening and speaking. The object of those faculties is Jesus himself, the living and incarnate Word of God.

Baptism: The Genetic Code of Opening

It is surely instructive that Jesus first, then the Church throughout the centuries in the baptismal rite, would use the word *ephphatha,* "be opened." It suggests that the real suffering of the human soul is somehow linked with being closed.

To close up, like a porcupine, is a natural reaction to feeling or actually being threatened or attacked. It can be the reaction to those gratuitous wounds mentioned above, inflicted on us by other human beings, sometimes even by those closest to us, without any fault on our part. I suppose that all of us have received such wounds in the fray of married, family, social and even Church life, and indeed from our most tender years. I also suppose that each of us, sometimes gratuitously and at other times out of anger or revenge, has hurt those we love.

Seventeenth-century philosopher Thomas Hobbes might have included this crazy tendency in his syndrome of *homo homini lupus,* "Man is a wolf to his fellowman."[1] He concluded that society had to be organized on the basis of the principle of self-defense so as to keep the "wolf" in the other at bay. Such an approach may seem realistic, but it is certainly pessimistic, for such a society will remain essentially closed, as will its marriages and families, surviving only by a mutual contract not to kill one another!

How different is the vision of Jesus! He offers a whole new understanding of man and woman as individuals, as married people, as family, as society, as Church and as world. It is a vision contained, as if by genetic code, in his programmatic prayer, "Ephphatha... Be opened!"

Being open requires attitudes and virtues of courage and trust on the part of each and all. But more important, it requires, and will receive, the power and grace of the visitations of Jesus. If on our side we loosen the bonds that shackle us to our dysfunctions and unleash the powers of our pain, hurt and groaning, Jesus will visit us and absorb our bleeding. He will heal us of being closed in upon ourselves and make us open to one another and to him.

Glorious Wounds

Undoubtedly, we must first recognize that indeed we do hurt. We will say all too quickly, "I have no real pain in my life," even though our hearts are bleeding. We easily bury our pain deep in our psyche and in our hearts, often precisely because it is so great.

Think of a child who feels unloved by his parents. He will say, "How can my parents not love me? How can I think such a thing? How ungrateful of me!" And so the pain of no love is made worse by the pain of denial and guilt. As the child grows, the pain grows too and expresses itself in problems ranging from addiction to murder.

Since we so easily bury our wounds, we may need help seeing them and feeling distress over them, groaning and grieving over them. Likewise, since we often do not remain alert to the visitations of Jesus, we may need help sensing his loving power within us, hearing his groaning deep within us. For indeed, our Jesus is a loving Savior who groans in empathy, sympathy and compassion for our pain. And what does he groan? *"Ephphatha...* Be opened, that I might heal you and make you whole!"

We need to encourage one another and to seek together the genetic code of openness. Christian resources, human and spiritual, are available. We need to have the courage to prioritize them in time and money. The healing of hearts, the opening of hearts, will be the source of healing in marriages, families, society and, indeed, those aspects of the Church's life that seem not yet fully open to the Savior.

Vulnerability is frightening. Unless we are prepared to stay vulnerable with each other, our fate will be the hurt and anger of isolation, even in the midst of a big family, a big city, a big Church.

In the Book of Revelation the wounds of the Lamb of God are seen glorified in heaven. Our wounds can kill us, but if we let them be opened to the Lamb, they too will become our glory.

Let us groan in prayer with Jesus, that the whole of our person, body and spirit, may be opened to his healing power. Let us pray that our isolation and our imprisonment within ourselves, our families, our society and even our Church and world may be ended. Lord Jesus, in your great mercy, hear my groaning and cry out within my soul, *"Ephphatha...* Be opened!" Amen.

On Reflection

Baptism is both gift and task, a "genetic" grace that we will waste if we do not live it out. Do I even realize what it means to be baptized?

Has Jesus' *ephphatha* to me fallen on deaf ears? Am I afraid to speak, defend and praise his name?

Where the experience of life has closed me up, how can I truly groan for the help of Jesus to open me up once more?

Where does Jesus' authoritative voice again need to cry, "Be opened!" in my life? Is it in my marriage, in my relationships, in my prayer?

Might I cry out *"ephphatha"* to God himself? What would I mean by that?

✠

Merciful Redeemer, I groan before you day and night. Make me alert and vulnerable to your closeness, to the healing touch of your Spirit. Open the eyes, ears and voice of my heart to be filled with the light, the sound and the praise of your healing compassion!

Open me up to your visitations, be they the permanent ones of baptism and confirmation or the fleeting ones of the moment. Open me to your body, the Church. Open me to the truth of my neighbor. Open to me the gates of holiness and of heaven that I may enter and give you thanks! *Christe, eleison.*

CHAPTER ELEVEN

The Body of Merciful Love

Corpus Christi. Amen. (The Roman Missal)

A men is our response to the person who administers the Blessed Sacrament to us. It comes from the Hebrew term for "truth." So we are saying, "In truth, I believe this is the Body of Christ."

Hence we are not saying *amen* to a mere symbol nor, as some have argued more subtly, to a reality only if the one receiving it believes it to be so. Nor is it the Body of Christ only for as long as the Mass lasts. No, our *amen* is the response of faith to Christ's own words: "This *is* my body.... This *is* my blood" (see Matthew 26:26-29). It brings us up, so to speak, to Christ's level of commitment, of meaning, of sincerity in what he says and does.

True, the *signs* of bread and wine are just that, *mere signs*, but they become sacramental when, through the words of consecration the priest pronounces in the liturgy, they bring about the grace they signify. That grace, that divine reality underlying them, is the glorified Lord Jesus himself: body, blood, soul and divinity. Were a church building to fall upon all in it and kill them, the Body and Blood would remain so long as the external signs, or "species," remained.

Such is the loving commitment of Jesus to us; such is his desire to be with us; such is his desire that we would be with him. Our *amen* reaches much deeper, however, because the sacrament of the Eucharist invites us much deeper.

Oneness of Flesh, Memory, Love

Our own human body is the first thing we experience, in its fascinating aspects and in its less fascinating aspects. Through the body our conscious mind begins to develop by means of the relationships of those who care, and even of those who fail to care, for us. The mind and the faculties of the soul, at least initially, need the senses to develop. The body challenges the soul, even struggles with it for domination.

Awkward adolescence is a time of great potential for the body to be formed by the values of the soul. The vigor of youth enables the mind and heart to develop with intensifying rhythm. This vigor is wasted when the body and its needs and caprices lay low the flame of the soul.

The onset of age, sickness and mortality bespeak the decay of the body but also, for many, the refinement of the soul in love, suffering and wisdom. The body carries with it the memories of the past, not just of the surgical incisions but also of the long hours in the sun or at work, the long years of depression or anxiety, the long years of sickness, weeping and suffering or indeed of rejoicing and genuine love.

Letter-writing, E-mails, telephone calls are all good ways of being in touch without being able *to* touch. It is *physical presence* more than anything that makes us feel the love of the other. We harbor the desire to see the faces that are gone, to touch the hands that once caressed, to embrace the body of one whose love was communicated by his or her very way of walking. Particularly loved is the human face, fascinating in its ability to communicate—and to hide. An ethnic group, a race, a people, are identifiable because they live or lived in the same place. Physical proximity is the raw material for social oneness, although at times it can lead to strife.

Corpus Christi: the Body of Christ. At its minimum this is the sacrament of the physical proximity of Jesus to us. It is the sacrament of Christ's fidelity to the incarnation of his divine Person. It is the memorial of the extremity of love with which he loved us.

We may stretch our eyesight through telescopes or other instruments as far as the outer galaxies to see if we can catch a glimpse of him at the right hand of the Father. But he has chosen a far better way, a way that permits him to be with the Father and yet to be with us. That way is the Eucharist: God still among us, always among us until the end of the age.

And in that sacramental Body—which we contemplate momentarily in our hand, or on our tongue, or more at length behind the tabernacle door or exposed in the monstrance—we are not seeing a symbol. The Eucharist is like a window into heaven itself, a window that becomes ever more transparent the more we allow the Body of the Lord to become our own body, the more we allow our own bodies to become his. We commune with him in Communion so as to be transformed into him as he is being transformed into us.

This is the grace of the Eucharist: communion, becoming more fully one body with the Lord and with one another. That is why *the Eucharist creates the Church*, and the Church, in witnessing to the Body of the Lord, draws people toward him. This is what the Second Vatican Council meant when it spoke of the Church as the "sacrament...of the unity of the whole human race."[1]

Heart of the World

So there is much to adore in the Body of the Lord. As you allow your eyes to become fixed upon that little white host, think of the eternity that lies behind it. Think of the vast universe, which sooner or later will be drawn into that host, for judgment unto life or death.

Think of the body of him who was truly born of the Virgin Mary. Think of all he went through as a child, an adolescent, a youth, a young adult—like us in every way except sin.

Think of the hands that blessed the children and healed the sick; of the voice that calmed the storm and called Lazarus from the tomb; of the eyes that pierced with love the heart of the rich young man, that saw Nathaniel and Matthew from a distance before calling them to leave everything and follow him.

Think of those feet that walked mile after mile to preach the good news of salvation: "God is with you, for *I* am with you!" Think of his smile, his singing voice, his angry and majestic voice, his tearful cries, his gentle whispering.

Think, finally, of his passion and of the marks it made on his body, those same marks that are now glorified, that we now receive in the sacrament of the Eucharist and that one day we shall behold with our own eyes if we live and die in his love.

As your heart is drawn into his through contemplation of the Eucharist, draw to your own heart the millions of people suffering in millions of ways. For them the Body of the Lord will be their eternal healing and salvation.

Remember those who curse him, reject him, despise him. Allow your own heart to feel something of his pain. Perhaps God will use your life to draw some of them to bless, accept and adore him.

Pope John Paul II calls the Eucharist the "heart of the world."[2] Who among us does not want to say *amen* to that— to be in, to beat with, that heart? Let our resounding *amen* lead us to seek time to love and adore him in the Eucharist. Let us move on to find healing, peace and inner unity. Let us come to understand deeply how the heart of Jesus beats with eternal, crazy love for this passing, crazy world in which we are but pilgrims.

"Corpus Christi. Amen."

On Reflection

When all is said and done, do I share the faith of the Church in the real presence of Jesus Christ in the consecrated bread and wine?

How does this faith affect my life?

Christ is present in many ways to us. What is so special about his real presence in the Eucharist?

How committed is my devotion to the Eucharist? Do I take it for granted by receiving it unworthily? Do I prepare myself adequately to receive it? Is my *amen* from the lips or from the heart?

How does the Eucharist define my relationships with others?

✠

Merciful Jesus, how can I thank you enough for the immense humility of your Eucharist? I give myself body, blood, soul and humanity to you, as you give me your body, blood, soul and divinity. You make me a living tabernacle; you receive even my flesh into your own dwelling place.

Fill me with the intimacy of your glorious body, present in the host and in your bride the Church. Set my heart within your Eucharist, that I might know myself at the heart of the world and love it with the love of your own heart. Amen! *Kyrie, eleison.*

CHAPTER TWELVE

The Bread and Breath of Life

When it was evening on that day, the first day of the week, and the doors of the house where the disciples had met were locked for fear of the Jews, Jesus came and stood among them and said, "Peace be with you.". . . When he had said this, he breathed on them and said to them, "Receive the Holy Spirit." (John 20:19, 22)

The disciples were afraid of death. That fear would be their master no matter where they might hide. But if someone stronger than death were to break its chains and pass through the walls and doors of their fear, then that someone would be Master of death and liberator of all who fear death. And someone did, in fact, accomplish that: His name is Jesus the Christ, the Son of the living God.

For him there are no locked rooms, no tombs. Because he is sinless, he is deathless. To each one of us, as to the astonished apostles, he says: "Do not be afraid. I am the first and the last, and the living one. I was dead, and see, I am alive forever and ever; and I have the keys of Death and of Hades" (Revelation 1:17-18).

Inside the Castle

The "peace be with you!" of Jesus interrupts the flow of fear's logic; he pierces it from the inside. Just as he destroyed death by dying, so he comes triumphantly and stands inside the locked room of every fearful heart, instilling everlasting joy.

Saint Teresa of Avila compares the soul to an interior castle.[1] Probably no one is without one or another locked room, or reserved floor, in his or her castle. There are many fears locked in the human heart. Some are born of great pain caused even by those who would be closest to us. Others are born of sin, of an unwillingness to be open to God or neighbor, to give and receive and even to be healed. But ultimately all our fears come down to one: the fear of death.

The sting of the tragedy here is not so much that we *will* die, for we certainly shall; it is that we can live pretending we will not. This self-invented immortality is the work of evil in us. Indeed, deception is evil's most classic tactic. Fake immortality is an illusion, one that death is glad we espouse. It keeps us from finding the Way, the Truth and the Life.

But Jesus is neither daunted by our barricades nor deceived by evil's tactics. Never! He comes and stands triumphantly within and shows the wounds of his love. He shows how deeply he holds us in his heart. In the locked rooms of every interior castle, Jesus continues to show those same glorious wounds.

Jesus breathes on the disciples, giving them the Holy Spirit to forgive and to retain sins. The heart of his mission, and thus the apostolic mission, *is* the forgiveness of sins. We need to shake ourselves to remember that our sins pierced open the heart of God. Jesus expired from God's own depths his very breath of life so that we might be forgiven and have life in his name. Before he died he gave his Body at the Last Supper as our *bread of life*. After he rose, he gave his Spirit of forgiveness as our *breath of life*. Both are exquisite gifts of the exquisite love of the exquisite Redeemer. Both he entrusts to the apostles to be handed on to all who, although not seeing, would yet believe in him.

Just as we are united in the body of Jesus, through the ministry of bishops and priests, by partaking of Holy Communion, so we are reconciled in the body of Jesus, through their ministry, by participating in holy reconciliation. We cannot and must not separate these two, the Bread and the Breath. The more we sincerely grow in love for the one, the more we will grow in love for the other.

The fresh bread of the Eucharist and the fresh breath of reconciliation are like the body and soul of faithful Christian living. Just as no one can sit at home and make the Eucharist for himself, so no one can sit at home and make reconciliation for himself. Jesus chided Thomas for not believing in the witness of the apostles; would he perhaps chide us for being slow to believe in their power to forgive sins?

Until he returns in glory, Jesus' love wants the words of the priest to make him truly present in the bread and wine of Communion. He also wants the words of the priest to make the Holy Spirit of power and forgiveness truly present in confession, breathing into every last room of our interior castles. No priest consecrates bread and wine or forgives or retains sins on his own authority or by his own power or because he is better than anyone else. He does these things only in the power and authority of Jesus living in his body, which is the Church.

What is more, no priest *is* a priest on his own authority but only by the call of Jesus in the Church. Once ordained a priest, he is no longer just some man. However unworthy he may be in his own heart, he is consecrated in the holiness of

Jesus the Priest and sent to you to act in the person of Jesus, to speak the words of Jesus, to serve the sacraments of the love of Jesus to his bride the Church. Surely this is what the parish is all about!

Victorious Words

Just as Jesus forgave the good thief, the adulterous woman and the apostle Peter, so Jesus through your priests forgives you with a certainty and definitiveness that are stronger than death and hell. The power of absolution is the power of resurrection. It is a re-plunging into the waters of baptism. Jesus recreates the heart sick with sin and broken with sorrow and holds it within the embrace of his Cross, the embrace of God himself.

How many times have we heard of the power of absolution, of its freeing and dignifying effects? Absolution restores our hearts to hope, confidence and trust. It enables us to bring forgiveness into our relationships, our marriages, our homes; gives impetus and direction to our choices; calms the gnawing anxiety of guilt and depression; mends what is broken and alienated within us; reinvigorates our souls with the desire for the kingdom of God!

We must neither accommodate sin nor compromise with it, not one cancerous inch. But only his almighty mercy can enable us to resist sin. How can we refuse or be lukewarm toward such a strong hand stretched out to us?

Saint Faustina, the saint of Divine Mercy, is a good intercessor for us. Let's pray often, with simple and humble faith, for our priests' ministry of reconciliation. The peace of Jesus and the joy of the apostles are for every interior castle. In the sacramental intimacy of individual confession, let us be open to hear those simple, victorious words of the priest: "I absolve you from all your sins in the name of the Father and of the Son and of the Holy Spirit. Amen."

On Reflection

Do I fearfully lock the sacrament of confession out of my life?

What prevents me from seeing it as the most powerful means of interior liberation that exists?

What is the relationship between the Bread and the Breath in my life?

Do I fear the forgiveness of Jesus because I don't want to admit my sins?

Is lukewarm belief in the sacrament of confession due to a weak understanding of Christ's relationship to the Church? Why does Christ forgive through the ministry of the Church?

What could encourage me to renew my faith in, and practice of, confession?

✠

Merciful Son of the Father, breathe once more upon your Church and on the hearts of all believers, that we may be refreshed by the grace of confession. Free us from the inane fear of revealing our spiritual brokenness to your priests, the ones you have chosen to be the missionaries of your sacramental forgiveness. May your presence fill us with joy and confidence to welcome your liberating love. Let those victorious words, "I absolve you from all your sins. Peace be with you!" resound in our hearts. *Christe, eleison.*

CHAPTER THIRTEEN

Divine Mercy

Jesus said to them again, "Peace be with you. As the Father has sent me, so I send you." When he had said this, he breathed on them and said to them, "Receive the Holy Spirit. If you forgive the sins of any, they are forgiven them; if you retain the sins of any, they are retained." (John 20:21-23)

I do not intend here to explain why the Second Sunday of Easter has come to be named "Divine Mercy Sunday," nor to recount the inspiring story of Saint Faustina. I prefer rather to sound aloud the bugle. This is in obedience to what Jesus once said to Saint Faustina: "Priests are to tell everyone about My great and unfathomable mercy."[1]

Here I will reflect on only one of mercy's resplendent qualities. It appears frequently in Saint Faustina's writings. It is, I feel, the key to opening one of the most stubbornly closed doors in the human heart—namely, our crazy distrust of the mercy of God as Jesus has revealed it to us.

The key quality of which I speak is faithfulness, the unfailing availability of divine mercy to all. God is inexorably merciful. Mercy is "love's second name,"[2] and Jesus is "Love and Mercy itself."[3]

A Bad Hangover

Often our distrust of mercy is not a clear-cut attitude but a vague and heavy spirit of resistance, a gnawing reluctance.

And while we would rather be free of that attitude, and so know deep peace, a number of things stop us.

For one thing, we procrastinate. We try to tell ourselves the attitude will go away, like a bad hangover. We are reluctant to let go of the things that cause it. We feel shame and frustration at not understanding our own humanity. We are angry at our own foibles and still angrier that we have to admit them, even to ourselves—never mind to God, not to speak of the priest.

One way or another, many of us get like this. The problem is that this heavy spirit of resistance is like a bad cold. If left untreated, it turns into a kind of spiritual SARS. It becomes a dark, deep and deadly distrust if we rationalize it and try to justify ourselves. And it infects others very easily.

We start calling evil good, and good evil. We attribute to our own conscience an infallibility that we would deny even to the pope. We blame the Church for giving us guilt complexes, for being out-of-date in its moral doctrine. We make a convenient yet spectacularly artificial separation between Christ and the Church, as if Christ had decided to dispense his graces without her. In effect we say, "Christ, yes; the Church, no."

We blame our parents, living or dead, not just for our hang-ups but for our indecisiveness in dealing with them. We blame our siblings, teachers, the government. We blame, we blame! The very aspect of our face comes to communicate self-righteous blame, and our actions and words smell of it, like hard liquor on someone's breath.

At the root of our resistance lie the mystery of iniquity and its fatally clever conniving. It is pride that resists admitting guilt and creates an inner fantasy world, a spiritual

Disneyland where we play at life, leaving the challenges of reality and maturity outside. We fear the pain of renouncing our fantasies in order to embrace true healing. Pride flourishes in distrust—and ends in despair. In an amazing show of manipulation, it convinces us that we are being coherent when we contradict ourselves.

While pride persuades us that our sin is too big for divine mercy and our humility more breathtaking than Christ's humiliation, it also tells us that we are too important and too tragic to accept the fact that by merely saying "I'm sorry" we could be restored to God. Pride would have us believe that we are beyond right and wrong, grace and sin, redemption and perdition, God and the devil—indeed, beyond Christ, Church, sacraments, heaven, hell and humankind itself. These all mean nothing when pride has its way.

If you find yourself thinking and acting like this, you may be lingering on a sorry path to nowhere. Thomas wanted proof of the Resurrection; Judas would simply have had no interest in it. Much of civil society and some of our lawmakers and law-caretakers would simply look the other way if the risen Lord appeared to them to say this or that law or scientific project was not the way to go. Behind the personal and societal loss of the sense of true, objective morality lies a cancer of the soul: distrust of divine mercy.

How the Phoenix Arises

But how can I seek divine mercy if I believe I can do no wrong? How can I appeal to conscience to excuse myself from obeying the truth, when if Truth in person were to speak to me, I would ignore him? If science is the new dogma, if technicians are its high priests and physical well-being the only, or principal, criterion of morality, why pay lip service to God?

In such a world it is no surprise that God should be kept out; indeed, it becomes an imperative to get him out, be it of the oath of allegiance, the national anthem, the dollar bill or the classroom! The false understanding of the separation of church and state leads to the elimination of God and, ultimately, the self-destruction of the state.

But the cold of eliminating him is far better than the lukewarm pretending to do him homage and then flatly provoking him to his face: "What you do with your mercy is your concern; what we do with science is ours!" Distrust of divine mercy manifests the devastating effect of sin in the human heart.

Can the phoenix arise from such devastation? Can my crazy distrust of the mercy of God be discarded so that I can have life? Can the Church and society speak of and to God with its heart and actions on fire, not with cold or lukewarm lips?

The answer is yes! And the power to say and mean yes is Christ Jesus our Lord. As if to prove how well he loved us, he absorbed in his own humanity our sins and afflictions. He died for us while we were still sinners and rose for us that we might become just and holy in him. His act of love for sinners is definitive and irreversible. On the cross he spoke of our craziness: "Father, forgive, for sin has made them crazy. They don't see what they are doing" (see Luke 23:34).

On the cross Jesus accepts us in our very act of rejecting him. He says, "I forgive you; peace be unto you." He confounds the logic of pride with the wisdom of mercy. He takes the power out of sin by forgiving it.

We no longer have to cling to our shame before him, for it is no more! In the beautiful words of Saint Augustine, "…What is mercy but a certain feeling of compassion in our hearts, evoked by the misery of another and compelling us to offer all possible aid?"[4] Mercy is the heart of our relationship with God and each other.

We can always hope for God's mercy. There is no situation of moral or spiritual misery, however grievous, from which the mercy of God in Jesus cannot rescue us. His mercy hounds us, seeks us. Like rays of light seeping through the cracks around the closed door of a darkened room, his mercy draws us to that door. From the other side he is gently calling and knocking in the hope that we will open to him.

His mercy is unrelenting, unabated, ever persistent, faithful, always vigilant. Like the air we breathe, like the very consciousness we have of ourselves and of our beating hearts, divine mercy is simply always there.

Mercy is revolutionary in that it renders rebellion and duplicity meaningless. Jesus turns sin against itself by making it a chance for the sinner to experience the depth of his love. This does not mean that we should sin so as to know his love. Think of Our Lady, the sinless virgin who knew God's love to the full. Mercy justifies us but not our sin. Knowing that mercy is available means that we need not feel cornered or checkmated by sin.

Moreover, divine mercy does not exist in the abstract: It's not a thing. It is the powerful bond of spiritual love born in the personal encounter between the faithful God of compassion and the sinful human being. Mercy recreates our unsullied relationship with God, passing first and necessarily through the Church and through Jesus. The entire treasure of divine mercy subsides in the flesh of Jesus, poured out for us on Calvary, transmitted to us across the centuries by the Holy Spirit through the ministry of priests in the confessional and at the altar.

Pope John Paul II calls the Eucharist "a great mystery, a mystery of mercy"[5] but explains that Communion requires sacramental confession, at least for those who are conscious of mortal sin. This is so logical in the supernatural realm! No one's rights are being violated; rather, no one's sin is being blessed.

How can I be truthful in receiving Holy Communion if my life in Christ's eyes—which see me through the Church —is sick with the deceit of mortal sin? If my soul is not disposed to receive mercy and I am not willing to change my life according to the demands of mercy, how can I sincerely receive the Body and Blood of Christ? To take Communion in such a state is to partake unworthily of the Body of the Lord and to aggravate one's own sinfulness (see 1 Corinthians 11:27-30). And yet the beauty of mercy is that I can, in sacramental confession and if I truly repent, receive complete and total forgiveness even of that terrible mistake.

The mystery of mercy in the Eucharist and in the sacrament of reconciliation calls me to maturity and seriousness in all my relationships. And as is true in any solid relationship of love, maturity and commitment can be built only on the solid rock of unconditional trust.

Miracles of Mercy

Strangely, we may fear to approach the overwhelming beauty of divine mercy. We fear the tears that unleash the terrible pain and absurdity of our own sin, buried tragically inside.

We hold back from confession despite the fact that sin itself is the source of that pain. Sin is what saps our strength and energy like a parasite, steals our peace, wipes joy from our countenance, frays our temper and our nerves, disturbs our sleep.

God himself weeps with us, with divine tears of compassion. Jesus wept at the sins of Jerusalem; he wept to be delivered from death. God's mercy empathizes with us and enters into our suffering. We are not alone in our suffering, nor are we condemned to suffer forever.

This fact brings forth our own tears of relief from the tensions we build up in our fearful hiding from others, from God and even from ourselves. The tears of admission and confession flush out the chaotic waters of sinfulness and leave our hearts open to the living waters of divine mercy, which will restore all those things stolen by sin. How many marriages and homes would be preserved and strengthened if we had but the courage, the simplicity and the trust to pour forth our pain, sorrow and guilt before the heart of Jesus and so learn to forgive one another!

So do not be fearful when approaching Jesus. It is in the confessional that "the greatest miracles take place," and these miracles "are incessantly repeated."[6]

Perhaps the greatest of these miracles is the ability, even after long years of sorrow and pain, to pardon myself in the strength of divine mercy. Trying to forgive myself on my own does not satisfy my need to confess, and self-absolution does not remove my sins. I need acquittal before God, my Father, and the Church, my mother. And if I sin again, the Father, through the mother, mercifully and faithfully adapts his divine power to my faltering steps of conversion.

He gradually wears down my resistance to his peace. His mercy can never be outwitted, either by my self-deceiving vanity or by my self-condemning cruelty. It will not play game to the former, nor will the latter intimidate it. His mercy transforms the humiliation of sin into the humility of grace. It exorcises the ghosts of past guilt and breathes in the Spirit of refreshing forgiveness. It allows me to reinterpret my past life of shameful rebellion in terms of the unimagined opportunity given now for joyful obedience in the future.

To err is human; to forgive, divine. But we can never err in forgiving, for in being forgiven and in forgiving we become divine. Divine mercy's faithful persistence, its never-failing availability, restores hope to the desperate even if weakness leads to repeated falls. For no number of falls is more powerful or greater than the eternal readiness of God to forgive: No doubts or distrust can undo the faithfulness of God.

Jesus said to Sister Faustina, "[Let] the greatest sinners place their trust in My mercy. They have the right before others to trust in the abyss of My mercy."[7] Mercy makes it possible for us at least to creep gradually toward the ideals of holiness. Every little act of mercy, every attempt to show mercy will attract the lost, the abandoned, the lapsed back to Christ in his Church. Speak to others of the mercy of God; share with them your own experiences of that mercy; be divine mercy witnesses, apostles, secretaries, spokespersons.

"If the bugle gives an indistinct sound, who will get ready for battle?" (1 Corinthians 14:8). If our faith in divine mercy is weak, who will fight against sin?

For the lost to return to the heart of God, we must be strong and unflinching in our trust in that heart's mercy. So let the bugle sound loud and clear, and let the battle of the

Church of Christ continue until the King of Mercy returns to judge the living and the dead. He will reward with eternal life those who have lived, fought and died awaiting and trusting in his faithful divine mercy. "Blessed are the merciful, for they will receive mercy" (Matthew 5:7).

On Reflection

Pride is the enemy of mercy, inhibiting its being given or received. Why might I then resist mercy? Do I deny my pride by painting it as a right to privacy, as the freedom to do as I like or as nervousness in telling my sins?

Why do I postpone or simply rebel against the sacrament of confession?

Is private confession to God in prayer as good as sacramental confession? Is it easier?

Do I resent the fact that I must confess to a priest? Why?

How can I renew my faith in the mercy of God and in the means he gives for my sins to be forgiven, especially sacramental confession?

✠

Lord Jesus, by the power of your merciful passion, break through my resistance to your divine mercy. Grant me the Christian realism to accept the fact that I need, so very deeply, the refreshing grace of sacramental confession. Let me not separate you from your Church or your priests, for through them alone you have chosen to dispense the fruits of your Cross.

I will trust in your mercy at all times. I will call the bluff of my pride and its rule of mercilessness. Help me, good Jesus! Help me! *Kyrie, eleison.*

PART FOUR

Mercy and Life

For if you forgive others their trespasses, your heavenly Father will also forgive you. (Matthew 6:14)

CHAPTER FOURTEEN

From the Bottom of the Heart

I thank you, Father, Lord of heaven and earth, because you... have revealed [these things] to infants.... Come to me, all you that are weary and are carrying heavy burdens, and I will give you rest. Take my yoke upon you, and learn from me; for I am gentle and humble in heart, and you will find rest for your souls. For my yoke is easy, and my burden is light. (Matthew 11:25, 28-30)

On vacation we seek rest from work, from the often humdrum rhythm of daily life. That is good. But there are other toils and labors from which, if we are honest, we also seek deep and lasting rest. From these it is more difficult to find relief: worries, anxieties, anguish, fears, resentments, anger. We want relief from the many simmering, unresolved conflicts that lie beneath the surface of our "daily face."

Much of this toil and turmoil drives us to what might be called deficit living—the constant, nagging feeling that something is missing, that we are deprived. This can lead to an attitude bent solely on getting something out of everything for oneself, a form of self-centeredness. Our hearts become like bottomless pits into which we want to draw everything, not so much to love as to "get something out of it." Yet we know that our hearts really ought to be dynamisms that lead

us to give without counting the cost. We ought to have a sur-
plus way of living, not a deficit way.

So Near, Yet So Far

Jesus speaks to simple hearts, hearts that are little or infant
not in size but in attitude. These are the hearts that draw him
and to which he reveals himself and his Father. Indeed, God
himself is such a little One, a simple One, uncomplicated.

It is sin and its minions that create complications. From
the time when the serpent treated Eve to one of his more
famous question-and-answer sessions, we know that evil
thrives on self-indulgent cleverness, ambiguity and the
puffed-up self-sufficiency that these occasion.

Such a heart cannot receive Jesus, for Jesus just cannot
get into it: He doesn't fit. Yet Jesus can and does try to draw
such hearts to himself. He seeks to appeal to the delight of
such hearts, for he knows that, deep down, they want rest
and peace. They yearn to be free of their tortuous ways. And
so it is no coincidence that Jesus presents himself to us as the
Sacred Heart, meek and humble, source and promise of deep
and lasting peace.

The words of Jesus about himself in Matthew 11 fulfill
the promises of Jeremiah and Zechariah about the Messiah
(see Jeremiah 23:5-6; 30:8-9; 33:14-16; Zechariah 9:9, 17a).
The pierced heart of Jesus crucified, meekly bearing our
wounds and pains, gently and powerfully forgiving his execu-
tioners and the fellow crucified next to him, speaks to us in
terms so simple and direct that we cannot fail to be drawn to
him. He makes our yoke light, for he absorbs all its weight in
himself. He asks only that we bind ourselves to him in faith
and love so as to know his healing.

Jesus gently calls: "Come to me, all you that are weary!" (Matthew 11:28). Our problem is in the actual going to him. At any moment in our lives, Jesus cannot be any closer to us than he actually is. He doesn't just check in on us from time to time; his loving attentiveness is permanent, active and quick to take advantage of any opening we give him. We can at any moment move closer to him.

Yet sin in us produces the paradox that we fear that which we most truly desire. This is just what Satan wanted to happen to us in Eden. We fear being overwhelmed by the beauty and warmth of God. We are terrified at the thought of the divine intimacy. We are so near yet so far away.

It is the fear of death. But we must let go of this fear if we are ever to know eternal love. "Your steadfast love is better than life" (Psalm 63:3). We must die if we are ever to have the rest for which our souls long.

Jesus has given us many helps to come to him. Confession and Communion are two great highways that merge into one in him. Confession is a dying, a good dying, to the sin that distances us from him. Communion is a celebration of the "death of the Lord," by which we are united with his glorified body in heaven.

Yet we all know, at the level of our daily experience, that the greatness of these sacraments somehow does not seem to break through to the darker areas of our hearts. We believe in faith that they cleanse us and strengthen us, but often, and quickly, we feel that we are just the same, as if the grace was almost like water off a duck's back. Why is this?

What Is in My Heart?

While much of the darkness in us is due to our free choices for evil, some of that darkness results from pain and conflict that we have buried deep in our hearts. This pain, rooted often in the distant past, was so bad at the time that we preferred to pretend it wasn't there. Our response is like taking bad meat or fish and throwing it into the basement, locking the door, throwing away the key and letting it fester.

Buried pain does not die when it is buried alive. On the contrary, it somehow becomes more alive when we deny it. It grows and affects how we feel about ourselves, how we love, how we act. You can call this "basement" the unconscious or the dark regions of the heart. Whatever you call it, it influences the conscious or lighted regions of our hearts.

Untreated wounds lead us to build up all sorts of defenses. We put up an almighty *no entry* sign to the wounded areas, which we expect to be observed by the conscious part of ourselves, other people and, of course, the Lord. To live this way is to live, at least partially, a pretend life. We only live in one corner of our hearts, and we hope the rest will go away. This can lead to pretend relationships and even pretend religion. The superficial is as deep as we go, simply because then we feel safe!

Now all this is most understandable and merits our compassion and patience. But because it is understandable does not mean it is okay. I can understand that introducing a knife into someone's chest and pulling it down might lead to death, but understanding that does not heal it! What matters is that we try to clear out that basement with the light and the grace of Jesus, with humble honesty, courage and hard work.

We need not be afraid of surrendering our festering wounds to Christ: wounds of love lost or denied; wounds of dignity stolen, of integrity shattered by the greed of others, even of those from whom we most expected love and trust. Wounds need to be tended; they need the tenderness of God. Thus God revealed himself to Moses:

> The Lord, the Lord, a God merciful and gracious, slow to anger, and abounding in steadfast love and faithfulness, keeping steadfast love for the thousandth generation, forgiving iniquity and transgression and sin.
> —Exodus 34:6-7

Thus Jesus reveals himself to us as the Sacred Heart.

When we first grant Jesus entrance to our hearts, often we let him into the hallway, or maybe the sitting room, but not the basement! Yet he comes to bring the light and peace of his divine tenderness to our whole house, our whole heart. We cannot put on a good face for Jesus, even though he does love us for making some effort to be lovable.

If we cannot carry our own burdens, much less can we carry those of others. We need to let Jesus carry the whole lot of us. The yoke, the tie with him, is that we accept the fact— so easy, yet so difficult!—that he loves us with all our inner pain, conscious or unconscious. The lightness of that yoke is the uplifting and healing power of his tenderness, his gentleness, his humility and simplicity. The weight of our burdens lifts when we let ourselves be overwhelmed by God's humility and compassionate relief, revealed in the Sacred Heart of Jesus.

Read and Healed by the Word

But how do we do this? Prayer in all its traditional forms is one important step: prayer that is passionate, committed and seasoned with strong desires for holiness. But I urge on you another step that can help open up the basement of your heart.

God's Word not only reveals God to us but also reveals us to ourselves. The Word reads the one who reads it, and if the reader accepts the truth thus given to him, then the Word will heal him. If you want to know who you are personally in God's sight, you will find it in his Word. For his Word created you; it is the real genetic or genomic code. This means taking time to reflect on God's Word, day by day, and to allow to surface *from the basement* all those dark feelings that his Word seeks to enlighten and to heal.

Talk with him about your feelings; tell him even that you are afraid of bringing them to him. Take the gospel passages that most speak to your heart, for in them the Lord is seeking to get right down to that basement of your heart. Take a psalm and make it your own. There is a psalm for every feeling and mood of the human heart; the psalm expresses it in words worthy of God!

Coming to Jesus, in response to his invitation, "Come to me all you that are weary" (Matthew 11:28), is also this heart-to-heart encounter with the Word of God. Yes, this coming entails, in the first place, confessing your sins, receiving Communion worthily, praying, and practicing charity and virtue. But this other darkness within also needs to be brought specifically to him, to his Word and to his Spirit.

He will not fail to help you open up; his heart draws you to himself for this very reason. And as you accept the pain within you before his heart, he will free you of the labor and toil that have sapped your energy and broken your hope.

Make no mistake: To draw close to the heart of Jesus in this way, our own hearts must first be broken and surrendered to him. He takes out the heart of stone and gives us a new heart, a pure heart, a heart at rest in his own.

All this might frighten you, but remember how Peter walked over the turmoil of the deep sea and strong winds toward Jesus. The heart of Jesus is more powerful than all our pain and fear. Do not ever doubt the truth of this. But do not let that truth leave you complacent as you sink sweetly beneath the waves! Rather, cry out, "Jesus! Save me! Out of my depths I cry, depths I myself do not know, but which you do!" (see Psalm 130).

The world offers us easy options of superficial satisfactions, and great is the temptation to put off facing the real roots of our personal suffering and so court the oblivion of habits and attitudes that have only spiritual death as their reward. We need to keep the image of the Sacred Heart permanently before our eyes, minds, memories and imaginations, for only in him is life and salvation.

Begin calmly but courageously the bittersweet task of vacating the basement of your heart. To do this is to work for eternal life and rest. A beautiful hymn opens with "O Sacred Heart, our home lies deep in Thee!" Indeed, his home lies deep in us. He desires to pass today from the altar into the temple of our bodies, so that his heart may be the heart and center of all hearts. Is not this the ultimate longing of both God and humanity?

On Reflection

Lingering, painful feelings point to unresolved, painful situations or relationships. Why not take some time to reflect on them in the presence of Jesus?

Take a favorite gospel passage and ask Jesus to shed the healing and creative light of his Word upon your thoughts and feelings.

What might be the difference between the pain of unresolved memories and the pain of sin? How does Jesus respond to these two pains?

What can you do to overcome fear of the healing and intimacy of the Sacred Heart? Whose pain might you heal by a word of love, a gesture of kindness?

☦

Merciful Jesus, you give us the great grace of pardon from our sins but also of peace for our hearts. Through the wounds of your Sacred Heart, heal the wounds of my poor, sinful heart. Put fear to flight, instill confidence, inspire courage, ignite charity, excite joy, that I may love you and my neighbor in fullness from the bottom of my redeemed heart! *Christe, eleison.*

Attractive Distractions

Martha was distracted by her many tasks.... The Lord answered her, "Martha, Martha, you are worried and distracted by many things; there is need of only one thing. Mary has chosen the better part, which will not be taken away from her." (Luke 10:40-42)

Let us suppose you have just understood for the first time some aspect of the person of Jesus. You feel good, grateful, happy. You set yourself to savor it more deeply by reflecting with your mind and contemplating with your heart.

All of a sudden you see in your mind's eye the face of someone who badly offended you. All those wonderful feelings you had about Jesus fall away. You now feel resentment and anger. Your heart beats faster; your facial muscles tighten; you sigh and fidget. You also feel frustrated by the fact that you have been distracted. You feel bad because you have lost that consoling focus on Christ.

So you conclude, I cannot pray because I just get distracted. You may also conclude that Christ's reaction to you must be either one of tut-tut disappointment or of bare tolerance. You think that his love depends on how you feel or on what you understand about him.

"All Ears" for All of You

Martha and Mary are obviously two individual persons, but in most of us they are merged into one person. Just as each of us is the robber and the victim in the parable of the Good Samaritan, so each of us is also a mixture of the two sisters who welcome Jesus. At times we listen to him; at other times we are distracted, anxious and worried about many other things. We understand the annoyance of Martha; we would love to experience the apparent carelessness of Mary.

The Martha-Mary tension is the tension between action and prayer in the Christian life. It is the difficult challenge of keeping the vertical and the horizontal in balance. Like every tension, though, if handled properly, it can bring much life and fruitfulness, just as it has actually done in the life of the Church.

For example, we have active religious orders and more contemplative ones, neither of which is exclusively active nor contemplative. We have the "Our Lady approach": she pondered in her heart (see Luke 2:51). Then we have the "Saint Peter approach": he was ready to move (see Matthew 14:28-29; 16:22-23) and never shy about asking for clarification (see Matthew 15:15; 18:21; 19:27).

When you come to prayer, God's heart is stirred. He holds all creation in his hands, yet in prayer he is "all ears" just for you. But the you who goes to pray, and the you to whom God is listening, is the *whole* you, not just the part you consider more respectable, not just the *good* you. When you present yourself before Jesus in the Blessed Sacrament or in the quiet of your home, you are presenting to him *all* that you are, *all* that you carry in your heart, mind and memory; your experience in *all* the dimensions of your life, past and present. You present your body in its concrete reality, sick or healthy, in all its energies, from your sexuality to the blinking of your eyes. There *is* no other you! Just that one!

That real you is the one whose ID the Lord recognizes, loves, forgives and enriches with his graces. Of course, that Lord who is "all ears" for the real you is also a real Thou. He can no more present to you his "respectable" side than you can yours to him. He is real; you are real. The person of Jesus to whom you come is the same one who lay in the manger, ran in the streets of Nazareth, visited Martha and Mary and left a tomb empty. The you to whom he listens is the one whose *curriculum vitae* is written into the fiber of your consciousness and subconsciousness.

Prayer is not an escape from reality but a profound and personal immersion in it. Indeed, it is a call to be more real than you realize.

True Storytelling

In prayer, then, there is the encounter of two real persons, one human and one divine. In such an encounter two things at least are inevitable.

The first is that you come gradually to be truly present to one another. We speak of the real presence of Jesus in the Blessed Sacrament; but there is also the matter of your real presence to him in your own body and blood, soul and humanity. Real presence from our side takes time; you can't be fully present to someone in a flash.

Many people think they are really present to each other just because they are in the same room together and even talking together. But presence is not exhausted in the physical nor guaranteed by talking.

The second inevitability is that you both want to learn more about one another. Friends share things; friends in love share all things, freely and without reservation. That sharing comes through communicating, through telling one's story.

The gospel is Jesus' story, and we need to know and cherish the gospel with great dedication and zeal. "Ignorance of the Scriptures is ignorance of Christ."[1] How can I really relate to a friend if I do not want to know his story intimately and thoroughly?

The question then arises as to *your* story. In prayer it is surely good that we ask for what we need according to the will of the Lord. It is also true that our heavenly Father knows what we need before we ask him. But he still wants us actually to ask him, to show we trust him as a dear and generous Father.

He certainly seeks our worship in spirit and in truth through Jesus, his well-beloved Son, and in the power of the Spirit, who helps us in our weakness (see Romans 8:26). But God also wants to hear our story from our own lips. In telling him our story we come to understand ourselves in his sight. He leads us to know ourselves and so to love ourselves as he does.

God knows that we are reluctant to tell him our story. We are very conscious of our right to privacy, even before God. Our reluctance is usually about the down side of ourselves. Think of how good a face you put on your relationships even with your nearest and dearest. Likely you say to yourself at times, "If only they knew the whole truth about me!"

There can be at least three reasons for our reluctance to tell our story to Christ. One is that we are ashamed of some things we have done or are still doing. We fear his rejection. Shame has the diabolical, lying ability to convince us that God will indeed reject us if we speak our sorry truth.

Another reason is that, while ashamed of what we have done or are doing, we want to keep on doing it because we like it. Telling it as it is to Christ would mean telling him that we see no reason, we have no intention, he has no right, to stop what we are doing. In the words of Saint John, "The light has come into the world, and people loved darkness rather than light because their deeds were evil" (John 3:19). So we tell him tales; we create a fable and may even begin to believe it ourselves.

There is a third reason for some: They cannot tell Jesus their story simply because they do not even know it themselves. They have repressed it out of pain. They have chosen or been forced to forget it, and they live literally only on the edge of who they are.

That is a great tragedy, one that the Lord alone will know how to heal and redeem. Such people need encouragement to entrust themselves to the compassionate and all-knowing Savior. They merit great sensitivity and care on our part.

Capturing Thoughts for Christ

Whatever the reason for not telling one's full story to Christ, one thing seems very likely, even if surprising. The distractions that come to us in prayer, if not sent by the Lord himself, can always be made the object of prayer.

Why would the Lord send us distractions when we are doing such a good and holy thing as having deeper insights into him? It follows from what has been said that the Lord can do this because he wants us to tell him our story, all our story, not give him classes in theology. He loves us when we come to praise him, but he knows that sometimes we indulge in high spiritual escapades as a clever way of avoiding and confronting real problems in our lives.

It is natural to want to avoid and run away from difficult problems and feelings. But the more we do so, the less we will be able to deal with them, integrate them into our relationship with the Lord and, ultimately, have the courage and strength to see them through.

As in the example I mentioned at the beginning, the distraction of someone's face may bring back strong and unpleasant feelings of conflict and pain. Well, in prayer, Jesus wants to hear all about those feelings and that pain; he wants to hear all about that person, what happened, why it happened and how it can be brought to resolution in truth and charity.

If there is a face I do not want to see, I am actually hiding my own true face from Jesus. Jesus wants me to see that face until I can once again accept that person. For whether I like it or not, that person too is loved by the One I call *my* Jesus and will stand by his side and, hopefully, by mine in the kingdom of God.

Heaven is not exclusive, except of those who would make it so. Jesus brings us back from our spiritual fantasies to concrete reality in order to heal us and bring us peace. When love is real, fantasies are no more.

I am not suggesting that in prayer there will be a miraculous solution to your problems. I am suggesting, however, that there will be absolutely no solution to them if you do not yield them to Christ in prayer. In this sense your distractions can become your salvation. There is no distraction that we cannot expose to Christ. Saint Paul said, "We take every thought captive to obey Christ" (2 Corinthians 10:5).

Faith, trust and perseverance in welcoming distractions and surrendering them to him will eventually make your own story, however painful, a unique and powerful version of the gospel itself. Do not drop your jaw in disbelief at this, for this is the meaning of our baptism, of being Church, of being redeemed. There are no dusty corners in heaven for those who "just made it." There we all will be firstborn sons and daughters!

"The one thing necessary" of which Jesus speaks is, I believe, the willingness to focus all of one's life, good and bad, on the person of Jesus Christ. That does not mean that we move out of active life, as if life's horizontal dimension were not of God. Jesus did not ask Martha to stop serving; he asked her rather to motivate it by and to focus it on himself! We are to understand, evaluate and judge the horizontal in virtue of the vertical—that is, in light of our relationship with Jesus, which we render explicit in intimate prayer and fraternal worship.

There is no problem in the history of humanity, of each human person, that Jesus will not ultimately judge. It only makes sense, then, that by word and example, by prayer and action, we seek now to, draw ourselves, our activities and our relationships to Jesus. That is what Jesus wants of us and for us; that is "the better part" of our self-awareness before Christ and of our awareness of him.

Martha and Mary: Might we say *dis*traction and *at*traction? Both of these holy women later professed their faith in the divinity of Jesus as he raised Lazarus, their brother, from the dead (see John 11:21-27, 32). If we trust in the providence of God, our distractions, even in prayer, can be the doorway to greater attraction to the Son of God. Welcome your distractions, then. Leave your tomb and let Christ welcome you into his heavenly home.

On Reflection

Am I willing to explore my distractions in the light of the Holy Spirit, to understand what the Lord is telling me or asking of me?

Am I willing then to accept the full and true story of my life, also by means of the distractions I receive in prayer? Otherwise, why do I pray?

Jesus tells his story through the gospel, but it takes on a unique meaning for each person who listens to him. Do I give him time and space to reveal himself personally to me?

How intimately do I really know Jesus?

✠

Merciful Lord, your heart searches the depths of every heart to know and to scrutinize its secrets and its subtleties. When we flee from facing you in truth, you employ distractions to point us back to you. Make us patient with ourselves! Make us docile to your pedagogy of salvation! Make whole the countless fragments of our lives by attracting them to oneness in your heart! *Kyrie, eleison.*

CHAPTER SIXTEEN

The Contagion of Forgiveness

Peter came and said to him… "How often should I forgive? As many as seven times?" Jesus said to him, "Not seven times, but, I tell you, seventy-seven times."… "Should you not have had mercy on your fellow slave, as I had mercy on you?" (Matthew 18:21-22, 33)

On reading this text, the word *contagious* came spontaneously to my mind. There are many contagious things in life: contagious diseases, contagious fashions, even contagious events. Many contagious things can be good—for example, contagious laughter, which can transform a mediocre social moment into a memorable celebration of joy.

True, some people remain immune to what is contagious, good or bad. Somehow they are just not open to it. So why think of that word in relation to this gospel text?

You could sum up Jesus' message to Peter about forgiveness, and the parable that goes with it, in the following statement: Forgiveness, to *be* forgiveness, has to be contagious. Jesus teaches us the same thing in other, more familiar words: "Forgive us our trespasses as we forgive those who trespass against us" (see Matthew 6:12). One's request for forgiveness proves sincere only when one is able and willing to forgive.

A Pathetic Question

The previous section of chapter 18 of Saint Matthew's Gospel deals with fraternal correction. What can we do to get a brother to admit he needs to be forgiven? In the text quoted above, however, Jesus teaches the only Christian reaction toward one who makes that admission, and that is, of course, to forgive.

It is interesting to note that it is Peter who asks this question of Jesus: "How often must I forgive?" Peter had his struggles with sin and forgiveness. In the end, the contagious mercy of Jesus won him over. Remember that painful moment, when you can almost feel Peter cringe, as Jesus risen asks him three times, "Simon, son of John, do you love me more than these others?"(see John 21:15-17).

In the episode we are considering now, Peter is still early in his "papal career." He asks how often one has to forgive anyone, as if forgiveness naturally had to have its proper limits! One might hear the underlying mumble of so-called human realism going on in Peter's head: "We can't have too much of this forgiveness business! We can't have the lawless and the scoundrel get away with too much! We need to be realistic! Somebody has to stop these people!"

Have you ever asked yourself how many times you've been to confession? Seven, seventy, seventy times seven, seven hundred? I know I have been countless times, and I'm glad to say that no priest ever put his hand up like a traffic warden to say, "Stop! Your seven times are up!" When I go, I expect forgiveness always to be given. I expect that hand to make the sign of the Cross. I come to hear those divinely comforting words of the priest, "I absolve you from all your sins."

Indeed, all of us know that forgiveness is always there to cleanse and comfort us, for Christ himself has promised it. Here's the catch: Forgiveness will always be there *if* I am prepared to *admit* my sins, *express sorrow* for them (that is, show some minimal realization that I have caused pain to God, others and myself), *try to make amends* for them (do my penance) and *resolve firmly* to avoid sins (that is, have real hope in the grace of holiness from the Lord).

So Jesus does not forgive sin unconditionally. Forgiveness is not the coward's naïve claim that one can just pretend evil is not there, or that it can be blown away by some spiritual puff of air. Absolution does not ignore sin; it destroys it by the greatest power ever known on this earth, the power of the death and resurrection of Jesus. For that power to work in us, we need to identify our sin (the famous examination of conscience), put it into words and spit it out.

The sacrament of confession is not an anachronistic ritual for the pious or scrupulous few. Absolution is infinitely more powerful than a nuclear missile, but the Lord launches it only to destroy well-defined targets, and he only does so through the ministry of his Church. The power of the contagious mercy of Jesus is directed to the single soul and the single sin, a power he breathed upon the apostles for the whole Church and for all people.

Some have said, and I am inclined to believe it, that Jesus would have died and risen to obtain the forgiveness of one single sin of one soul. Such is his love; such is the nature of his holiness, justice and forgiveness. Forgiveness is not a miserable, begrudging, finger-wagging, threatening "well, okay then." Forgiveness and mercy are of the essence of God's own being, as he himself declared to Moses: "The

Lord, the Lord, a God merciful and gracious, slow to anger, and abounding in steadfast love and faithfulness, keeping steadfast love for the thousandth generation, forgiving iniquity and transgression and sin" (Exodus 34:6-7).

In the face of this reality, Peter's question is pretty pathetic.

Is Forgiveness Possible for Me?

Another way of looking at the forgiveness given in the Church through the sacrament of reconciliation is to think of a blood transfusion. The sin-infected blood of our hearts is drawn out of us by absolution, and the life-giving blood of the heart of Jesus, which has been poured out for the forgiveness of sins, is fed into us. We are re-created by the blood of Jesus—that is, by the power of the Spirit, the Giver of Life, who creates within us a pure, renewed and steadfast heart. Blood is the symbol of life and purification in the Bible; the life and purifying power of Jesus is the Holy Spirit.

But here the idea of immunity comes to mind. Like the wicked servant in the parable, it seems at times that we are immune to forgiveness received. Why is that? Do we no longer believe in the power of Jesus to forgive, in and through the Church?

We limit our little "heart operation" to our private rooms for a host of reasons, ranging from sloth to spiritual blindness. But our sins are never private; they infect the whole body of the Church.

Could it be that we no longer believe in sin at all? After all, certain sectors of society now exalt as virtuous freedoms of expression so many things that it once defined as sins! That could make us think, "Well, times are changing. I am a modern person; I need to go with the flow." Or we simply could see in these changes a wonderful excuse for reneging on moral responsibility and indulging our puerile self-centeredness.

Could our immunity mean that we no longer believe in God at all? If there's no God, there's no moral law, so there's no sin. I am my own law—although, of course, I might choose from time to time to impose my law on others if their freedom gets in my way.

Yes, this immunity to seeking and receiving forgiveness could mean all these things. But there is one more thing that it could mean, and it is a very difficult thing to grasp because it is very elusive. Perhaps I may never seek forgiveness because, deep down, I cannot forgive myself.

I may think, "Why would Jesus ever on earth or in heaven want to forgive me?" This kind of thinking is pernicious, but it is a real attitude that can be at work deep down within us. I cannot forgive myself for my own darkness, and so I want no others, not even God, to tell me that they can.

When all is said and done, this is not a bad definition of hell. Hell is a place deep within my own spirit. It haunts me and frightens me, but somehow I am locked into it, perhaps reluctantly yet with some subtle approval on my part. On my own, I will eventually let my whole self be drawn into this hell, having thrown away the key.

The merciful God understands this terrible suffering of the human heart. He sees us hiding like Adam and Eve in Eden because we are afraid to be seen. It might have been the consuming fear of being seen in such pain that led Adam and Eve to leave Eden.

We are left in a hellhole similar to the pigsty of the Prodigal Son. The question is: Will I, like that son, remember my Father's house? Or will I, like Judas, remain closed in my fear of being exposed and judged but also forgiven, cleansed, renewed and exalted once more to the dignity of son?

The inability to forgive oneself becomes a wellspring of pain, which reaches beyond the spirit into the mind and body. In some cases its root might be terrible experiences of abuse (of any kind), of addiction, of sexual deviance, of the despair of ever being fully loved, accepted, healed.

What is the cause of divorce today? Could it be, among other things, that one spouse is struggling with this inability to forgive himself or herself? The result can be that sons and daughters, looking good and happy-go-lucky on the outside, are tortured on the inside because they do not breathe at home the contagious fresh air of forgiveness, understanding and compassion. Is this where drug addiction and alcoholism find their fertile ground? We often hurt, and hurt so badly, that we are afraid to open our hurt, even to the ones who love us, lest we be hurt even more.

Security systems, prisons and military force might well check or contain the ills of society. But only mercy, and only the mercy of God working contagiously through us, will truly heal these ills. This healing happens not just behind the confessional door, not only within the walls of the parish church, but in the intimacy of our marriages and families, in the ethos that inspires our schools, educational institutions and places of work.

Never Despair

Despair is the victory of the devil in a mind that freely embraces it. Despair has believed the diabolical gospel that evil is stronger than good, that Jesus was a fake and a failure and that good is the illusion of the weak and naïve. Despair is the greatest lie of the greatest liar. Despair is the sin of ceasing to hope for personal salvation from God, for help in attaining it or for the forgiveness of one's sins. Despair is contrary to God's goodness, to his justice and to his mercy, for he is faithful to his promises.

Without compromise we must send thoughts of despair back to whence they came: to hell. We need never despair of the forgiveness of God. His mercy in Jesus is our ultimate hope. It destroys even despair and beats evil's lying claims. Dying, Jesus destroyed sin and death; rising, he restored our life. That is the gospel.

The Church of Christ is the Church of mercy. We are that Church. Let us not be immune to his mercy but be wholly infected by it. Thus, by the power of his Cross, we can be merciful to one another and pray with sincerity and effectiveness to the Father of all mercies: "Forgive us our trespasses, as we forgive those who trespass against us."

On Reflection

Why is human justice not enough to resolve the ills of society?

When does my ability to forgive hit barriers? Why is that, and what are those barriers?

How can God's infinite mercy be reconciled with Church teaching on hell?

What is the relationship between mercy and truth?

What does it mean to be "smitten" by the mercy of God?

☩

Merciful Jesus, my heart cannot grasp the mystery of your mercy, but my heart can adore your mercy as a power beyond the capacities of any human being. Instruct my heart with the wisdom of your forgiveness, the wisdom of the Cross, that I may not limit your mercy within my human possibilities but be fully open to you, for whom everything is possible.

Lord, please rescue those in despair, that their broken hearts may find eternal hope and healing in the words of sacramental absolution. *Christe, eleison.*

CHAPTER SEVENTEEN

The Deep Waters of Mercy

He said to Simon, "Put out into the deep water and let down your nets for a catch."... When they had done this, they caught so many fish that their nets were beginning to break.... When Simon Peter saw it, he fell down at Jesus' knees, saying, "Go away from me, Lord, for I am a sinful man!"... Jesus said to Simon, "Do not be afraid; from now on you will be catching people."
(Luke 5:4, 6, 8, 10)

One of the worst effects of sin, if not its main aim, is to make us think that God stops loving us. It paints God as our enemy. Feeling bad about ourselves, we presume God feels the same way about us. And since sin is a regular feature of our lives, we can feel that God is never really happy with us. That "realization" can make us feel even worse. We sense that we are almost permanently distant from God. In turn, this can lead to resentment against God, the Church of God and the sacraments of the Church. "Why is it all so difficult?" we complain.

A next step might be simply to pretend there is no sin at all, that it's all a ploy by the clergy to keep us under control. Then we can either cut God and the Church out completely or transform them into what we want them to be.

That may entail, for example, making religion a spiritual security blanket or turning it into a pastime, like going to a concert or a museum. This, of course, is the real aim of sin.

Sin is not so much the illicit pleasure of the moment (which Satan would deny us if he could) as the long-term break with the true God and the deformation of true religion.

Jesus "Nets" Peter

God knows the tactics, the strategy and the objectives of sin. However, he has his own counterplan vis-à-vis the sinner. It is revealed in a special way in the gospel incident quoted above. Consider very carefully what happens between Jesus and Simon Peter.

Peter is minding and doing his own business, probably somewhat annoyed that his night's work has yielded zilch, nothing. Jesus, meanwhile, is fishing for believers among the crowd, which is practically pushing him into the water. Jesus knows the hearts of his listeners, but he also knows the heart of the man a few hundred yards away from him who is cursing his broken nets.

Quick on the uptake, Jesus approaches Peter, not yet directly, but through his boat. Peter was a practical man and would resonate with Jesus' request for use of the boat as a kind of pulpit. Maybe Peter thought he'd get something for the favor. Later he would, of course, beyond his wildest dreams.

Jesus gave priority to teaching the crowd, and only afterward did he speak to Peter. We can presume that Peter all the while had heard at least something of what Jesus was saying. We can also imagine his thinking: "This guy must have something good to say. Look at all these people. I must ask some of them what they think of him. They say he performs miracles: I could do with one myself after last night! Right enough, I like his way of talking: no mumbo jumbo, straight to the point, knows what he's talking about. I wonder what he's made of."

Whatever Peter's thoughts, there is no doubt that Jesus made an impression on him. And Jesus most probably knew it; otherwise it would have been off the mark for him to more or less command Peter to put out into deep water for a catch. In this command Jesus moves not just into Peter's boat but into his life, his work, his concerns and frustrations. Peter realizes it and, after a mild professional protest, does what Jesus asks simply because Jesus asks him.

It's not impossible that Jesus lent a muscular shoulder to help in the fishing. Why should we imagine him sitting majestically at the back of the boat? He was a practical man. There were apparently only two others with him in the boat, Peter and Andrew. So it is likely that Jesus would have worked hard with Peter and those involved in the expedition.

The abundance of the catch—think of the two boats almost sinking with the weight—speaks to the abundant generosity of Jesus. It also speaks to just how much he must have wanted Peter's faith and love. The abundance also speaks to the generosity of Peter's openness to Jesus. Notwithstanding the odds, he obeyed the word of Jesus, and Jesus rewarded Peter's trust in him.

So it was not just the boats that were full or overwhelmed: The heart of Jesus was also overwhelmed with love for Peter; and the heart of Peter was likewise overwhelmed with astonishment. Why astonishment? At the catch of fish, yes, but at much more. Peter somehow realized he was in the presence of someone holy, someone who manifested the power of God.

Like the prophet Isaiah at his calling, and like all human beings before the holiness of God, the natural reaction is one of awareness of sin. In becoming aware of God's holiness, I become aware of my own sinfulness. We all want to say: "Depart from me, Lord, for I am a sinful man."

This is the deep feeling of the soul to which I referred at the beginning: We sense distance; indeed, we strangely want distance from God. Jesus had commanded Peter, "Put out into deep water," and Peter commanded Jesus, "Depart from me!"

Drowned by Mercy

The response of Jesus to Peter's "command" brings utmost consolation. Jesus does not deny Peter's sinfulness. He does not say, "You have not sinned." He does much more.

First he sees Peter's humble confession. Peter fell at the knees of Jesus and confessed, "I am a sinful man." That very confession was the result of giving Jesus access to his boat, hearing the words of Jesus as he taught from the boat, obeying the command of Jesus and accepting the fact that Jesus was the power behind the draught of fishes. Jesus sees all this, and because of Peter's humility and faith he responds, "Do not be afraid; from now on you will be catching men."

Do not be afraid! Do not fear your sinfulness! Do not focus on your sins! Do not allow your sins to have the first or the last word in your relationship with me! Do not let sin attain its aim of separating you from me! Do not let your sin be more important than what I have just done for you! Do not let your many sins seem more than my generosity to you, my desire for you and for the faith and love of your soul! Do not let your sin get in the way of the great things I want you to do for me!

It is not sin that determines who you are; it is I! It is not sin that prescribes the direction of your life; it is I! Sin is not the authority in your life; I am! Sin is not your way, your truth or your life; I am! Sin is not your God; I am!

Yes, Jesus died for our sins, but that does not mean that our sins were the main purpose of his coming. *We* are that purpose! If sin infects us, Jesus heals us, not because he wants the sin that he removes from us but because he wants *us*—whole, holy, healed and happy with his own joy.

Sin may separate us from God, but it does not stop God from coming close to us. The separation sin causes is, as it were, on our side; but God is always near for those who wish to close the separation—that is, to repent. That is why Jesus calls the sinner.

Peter knew the gentle approach of Jesus, his ability to reach the heart with his Word, his desire to enter into Peter's life, his work, his company. Peter knew Jesus' readiness to show the fullness of his generosity in wonderful deeds. It is no wonder that Peter and his companions abandoned everything and followed Jesus. Never had anyone so completely reached into their hearts with such powerful yet tender love; never had they been so overwhelmed in their whole being and their whole lives.

In opening themselves to Jesus, despite their sins, they fell in love with him. They knew their lives would never be the same. They knew they would never understand themselves in the same way again. They knew that, although they had sinned, Jesus wanted *them*, not their sins, and that he would purify them from those sins.

Christ, Our Abundant Catch

This is Good News! This is the gospel! To be sure, we cannot deny the pain we feel when we sin, but that pain is nothing in comparison with the joy and solace that pour forth into our hearts from the merciful heart of Jesus. So to feel good about ourselves after we sin, there are two options: Either we deny that we have sinned and invent for ourselves a worldly happiness; or we confess our sins with humility and faith, trusting in the love of Jesus, and find joy in him.

If we try to handle sin and guilt alone, it will eventually destroy us, to the great sorrow of our merciful Lord. But if we come to him, especially in the sacrament of reconciliation, he will destroy our sin and exalt us in the joy of his merciful love. We can live genuine, happy and purposeful lives only if we allow Jesus to approach us personally and unite himself with us. Otherwise we may find some moments and experiences of passing jollity, but our hearts and souls will remain in darkness, lamenting and complaining.

To speak of sin, guilt, repentance and confession offends contemporary sensitivities. Certainly, some Church leaders have been guilty of using the doctrine of sin to instill fear and to manipulate people. It is good that we are freed from false understandings of these matters. However, freedom from false understandings of sin and its minions does not mean freedom from sin itself.

Indeed, this is perhaps the heresy of today: a false understanding not of sin but of freedom, a freedom from any responsibility to God. It's as if someone were to say, "You dare tell me I've sinned, and I'll take you to court. And if you insist, I'll take you to the Supreme Court to decide the constitutional meaning of the gospel!"

But it is Christ alone, and those to whom he has given his authority, who determine the true meaning of the gospel. It is Jesus himself, in texts like the one under consideration, and his dependable teachers of the faith who show us the true meaning of freedom. The Church shows us how Jesus interacts with the sinner to make him truly free.

Sin, alas, has its place, dark and destructive, and must be taken seriously. But we need always to deal with sin in the powerful presence of Jesus Christ, so that our trust and hope in him may deliver us from every evil and restore us to the glorious freedom of the children of God.

So put out into the deep waters of the merciful heart of God, and your abundant catch will be the joy of God himself.

On Reflection

Do I really believe that the forgiveness of sins is a doctrine of faith? Do I understand it? How can I better understand it?

Do I resist forgiveness? Whatever my answer, why is it so?

What corner of my heart longs to see the loving, merciful gaze of Jesus, my good and great Redeemer? What corner in the heart of my spouse, child, parent or neighbor longs to see my merciful gaze?

For what must I yet forgive myself?

✠

Merciful Jesus, grant me the deep and abundant waters of true spiritual understanding. Let sin not net me into despair. May I see it for what it is in my life and confess it as such. Let me see above all your merciful gaze. Let me be caught by you and know that, anchored in you, I need never again be afraid of evil. Make me a missionary of mercy, that I may make an abundant catch for you. *Kyrie, eleison.*

CHAPTER EIGHTEEN

Merciful Nostalgia

*That disciple whom Jesus loved said to Peter, "It is the
Lord!" When Simon Peter heard that it was the Lord,
he...jumped into the sea.... [Jesus] said to him the
third time, "Simon son of John, do you love me?" Peter
felt hurt because he said to him the third time, "Do you
love me?"... After this [Jesus] said to him, "Follow me."
(John 21:7, 17, 19)*

It is hard to know who was the more nostalgic: Peter or
Jesus. Given all that had happened to Peter, it seems almost
banal that he would still want to go fishing. But deep in his
consciousness, he and the others perhaps wanted to recapture
not so much the big number of fish as the experience of that
unforgettable morning, some three years earlier, when the
man from Nazareth first preached from the fisherman's boat.

At that time Peter had asked the Lord to leave him, for
he was a sinful man. Indeed, Peter was a sinner, and Jesus
did not deny it. Alas, it was on the night Jesus was arrested
that Peter's sinfulness became all too painfully clear.

Now, after the "Jesus matter" seemed to be over, Peter
still felt guilty about his denials. Perhaps he wanted to relive
the experience of Christ's forgiveness: "Do not be afraid; from
now on you will be catching people" (Luke 5:10c).

Peter felt a stinging nostalgia for that personal presence
and that compassionate gaze of the Master. He longed for
those words of mercy that had lifted his soul from depths

deeper than the waters of any ocean. With the memory of
thrice betraying Jesus still fresh in his mind, Peter was again
in those depths. He felt the dark of the night and its emptiness as he now went to fish again. He longed for Jesus to
come near once more and preach from his boat.

For his part, the risen Jesus knew of Peter's plight. Both
as man and as God, Jesus too would feel some manner of
nostalgia for his friends; their unfaithfulness did not make
him unfaithful. So he comes again to Peter. He comes to
renew his call in a way, in a place and at a time that Peter
would understand and that would fill his heart.

Free from death, Jesus comes to reinstate those he had
called at the beginning of his public ministry, now with the
power and authority of his resurrection. How good and con-
siderate Jesus is in the way he draws them back to himself!
He comes unobtrusively and fraternally, measuring the manifestation of his power in a degree that enables them to recognize him.

He eats with them, in a manner and with words that
would remind them of the Last Supper, the banquet of charity, the ultimate gift of his love. Jesus thus shows his own fond
memories of when he first called them and of when he last
left them, to die freely for their eternal happiness. They are
bound together in the memory of his love.

Peter's response to this is typical of the man and yet
filled with that strength and energy that come from knowing
that someone who loves you, literally to death, is near at
hand. Peter probably cannot believe that his nostalgic hopes
would be so wonderfully fulfilled by Jesus. Had Jesus asked
Peter to stand on his head, there is no doubt he would have
done so!

Unfinished Triple Symphony of Mercy

However, both Jesus and Peter know that there is some unfinished business to take care of. The other apostles need to know how things now stand between the Lord and Peter, in part, at least, that they might be able to put their full trust again in the one who denied Jesus.

As regards the one-on-one relationship between Peter and Jesus, it is possible that the two were already fully reconciled before this scene. First Corinthians 15:5 mentions an appearance of Jesus to Peter by himself.

Indeed, Jesus knows just how much Peter is hurting. He knows Peter's need to confess. And so Jesus comes to comfort him and above all to reassure him that the look Jesus gave him on that fateful night at the house of Caiaphas was indeed a look of total forgiveness. In that private encounter one can only imagine how Peter wept and how Jesus wept, for joy.

Of course, that encounter would have delivered Peter from the depths of spiritual darkness mentioned already. In that case, the fishing trip might simply be an expression of nostalgia and of hope that he would see the risen Christ again. Since we cannot know the exact sequence of the appearances of Jesus from the four Gospel accounts (and the account in 1 Corinthians 15), we need to see different possibilities for understanding Peter's behavior without being totally sure of which one is the correct one.

What we can say is that, in the collective encounter with the apostles on that morning by the lake, Jesus seems to want to restore and deepen the bonds between Peter and the others, as well as to show them that Peter is truly repentant and forgiven. Note that Jesus does not begin the conversation with any manner of remonstration. His approach is always amiable and generous, never scary and mean. Only after breakfast, after sharing together, does he ask Peter to speak up with courage.

Jesus' opener is a question about the intensity of Peter's love for him, not about the misery of his denials. It is the perennial question of God to every human being: Do you love me more than these others? Do you love me more than they love me, more than you love anything or anyone else, including yourself, more than you used to love me? Peter was already first in faith; Jesus now offers to make him first also in love.

But the word *more* suggests, well, more! It suggests a conscious choice and a constant growth; it stimulates renewed effort and perseverance; it fires a holy restlessness for Jesus; it is the stuff of holiness, of surrender and sacrifice, indeed of martyrdom.

It is also a question that instills great hope in the sinner. Here am I, says the sinner, so bad, so low, so sinful, so unworthy. But here is Jesus asking me if I will love him more than all the others! With this question Jesus seems to promise the sinner: It is because you have been so low, and yet have turned to me out of those depths, that I will raise you on high in the power of my love. When you were low, Simon son of John, you remembered the Peter in you, not the Judas.

Because of Jesus' question to Peter, all love for Jesus is now Petrine. The truth of Peter's faith *and* of Peter's love is now the matrix of our own.

Yet this threefold questioning by Jesus is also unsettling, distressing, as Peter plainly shows. He makes the link between it and his own triple denial, and it is precisely the third time that Jesus asks him the question that Peter feels the pain. The pain of repentance, deep and anguishing, is the pain of giving birth to love. It is a pain Peter would rather avoid, because it makes the memory of the sin all the more acute.

But Jesus, in his infinite knowledge of the heart, knows that unless a memory is faced, accepted and confessed, it cannot be healed. Sin is not to be glossed over but flushed out. The distress is not for distress' sake but because truthful openness needs to purge sin in its lying secrecy.

Jesus wins Peter over to this but at the same time encourages him to reach out for that "more," that greater love. Effectively, Jesus reveals to Peter that, by divine mercy, his ability to love is greater than his ability to sin. Jesus is repeating to Peter what he said to him when first they met: "Do not be afraid [of your sin]. From now on you will be catching people" (see Luke 5:10).

Pastoral Cadenza

In response to Peter's triple confession of "more" love, Jesus entrusts to him the task of feeding and caring for the flock. Indeed, unless an apostle loves Christ "more," he will be unable to feed the flock with the food it needs. Pastoral ministry, the task of the shepherd, is essentially to love Christ more than all else. It is to call all others to love him, to be lifted up from their depths, called back from their wandering. The more the shepherd loves Christ, the more he will feel empowered and fired to feed others with that love and, like the Good Shepherd, to lay down his life for his sheep, the act of supreme love.

This greatest love is precisely what Jesus promises Peter once his greater love has been confessed: When you were young, in those days of self-assertion and self-fulfillment, you did your own thing; but because you love me, you will, when you are older, be taken as was I and give your life for me and for the sheep.

When love for Christ has become the reason for one's life, nothing can be more logical than to give it up for his sake. His love is greater than death because it is better than life. When death is still on the stage of human life, what can there be in this life that can merit the unique treasure of our hearts?

This does not mean that we do not love the other gifts Christ has given us, but it does mean that nothing and no one beyond him can claim to be our alpha and omega, our all. Jesus said, "Whoever loves father or mother more than me is not worthy of me; and whoever loves son or daughter more than me is not worthy of me" (Matthew 10:37).

To prefer is precisely to "love more than," as Jesus puts it in his question to Peter. To cling to the realities of this life, in a way that denies Christ, implicitly or explicitly, is to return with the old Peter to the house of Caiaphas. All who prefer Christ to absolutely all else will and must also return to the house of Caiaphas—not with Peter but with Christ.

Most of us will not stand trial for our faith and love of Christ, but no one should doubt, even today, that the power of Christ, on the one hand, and the hatred of the world, on the other, will draw some to offer the ultimate sacrifice. When Jesus first called Peter, he made no mention of martyrdom. Now, however, in renewing that call, Jesus makes it plain to Peter that the gift of martyrdom will be given to him and asked of him.

Toward the end of our gospel scene, when Jesus says to Peter, "Follow me," Peter at last understands that the glory of Jesus is not to sit on the political throne of an earthly kingdom but to be crucified in loving sacrifice to the Father and to die for our redemption. To glory through the Cross, Peter must follow Jesus.

Our nostalgia for Christ is hopefully great, and he surely knows it. But his nostalgia for us, for the earth he walked and for the human race he so loves, is even greater. This love is manifest nowhere more completely than in the Eucharist. As we partake of the Body and Blood of Christ, Jesus asks each of us, not for the third but for the "nth" time, "Do you love me more than these?" (John 21:15).

No matter how distressful that question may be for each of us to hear and to answer, it is surely breathtaking and inspiring that "humble we" can satisfy the divine nostalgia by crying out from our depths, "Lord, you know everything; you know that I love you" (John 21:17).

On Reflection

Have I met Jesus in my own life? If so, what occasioned it? When and how did it happen? If not, what can I do to prepare the way for such an encounter?

Peter's first encounter with Jesus led to a lifetime of discipleship and to a martyr's death. What has my encounter with the Lord meant for my life and my death?

In the light of Peter's experience, does the attitude of Jesus to us change because we sin?

Can I let Jesus comfort me as well as challenge me? How do I answer Jesus' penetrating question, "Do you love me more than these?"

✠

Merciful Lord, you long for us to be aware of your presence, care and interest. The weight of our sins makes us doubt that truth, and our doubt lowers our expectations of you.

Make us mindful of your merciful encounters with Peter and of the change for the good they wrought in him. Help us bear gladly the hurt of your questions, since it is a hurt that heals and that blossoms in the surrendering of ourselves in love as your disciples. *Christe, eleison.*

CHAPTER NINETEEN

Healing Our Notion of Death

"Very truly, I tell you, unless a grain of wheat falls into the earth and dies, it remains just a single grain; but if it dies, it bears much fruit. Those who love their life lose it, and those who hate their life in this world will keep it for eternal life.... Now is the judgment of this world; now the ruler of this world will be driven out. And I, when I am lifted up from the earth, will draw all people to myself." (John 12:24-25, 31-32)

Throughout the war in Iraq, we have heard sobering statistics about how many have died. Indeed, among the many harrowing aspects of terrorism and war is the fact that they thrust upon us a keener focus on our own mortality.

We acknowledge what Saint Francis calls *sorella morte*, "sister death,"[1] only in an abstract way. We know it's there, we know it's coming, but we do not dwell on it.

In fact, for many people, for a good part of their lives, it is possible to feel immortal, even physically. When you are young, you can do what you like, for as long as you like, whenever you like. Yet all of us sooner or later must face the truth and face it personally: Death is ineluctable.

Philosophers, artists, musicians and psychologists will elaborate for us a whole variety of understandings of death. Some are dreadfully oppressive and depressing, some are palliative, and yet others are pragmatic, dramatic or satirical. But when all is said, sung and done, there is almost nothing more personal than one's own death and one's own acceptance or denial of its approach. Whether it comes suddenly or not, there is deep within the consciousness of the human spirit a realization that neither our love nor our heroism can deliver us from dying.

Masquerading Immortality

The times in which we live have to a great extent expelled religion from any relevance to society. And we need to ask ourselves honestly to what degree this is true, or we wish it were true, in our personal lives. But if religion—consciously or unconsciously, partially or completely—is excised like a cancer that consumes the energies of our *joie de vivre,* then religion's answers to the great questions of life are also cut away.

And the greatest of these questions is death. The power of technology and science can soothe that aching question only for so long; the joys of human existence can provide comfort for a time; but the masquerade of a pretended immortality must give way to the power of what it most denies. Without God or religion, death itself has the greater claim to immortality.

There is no use in inventing religion to kid ourselves; if we invent it, then it is just another ploy of our own self-deception. We can make a religion out of anything, but so long as it comes from humans it is no more than idolatry. When people make gods of themselves, however carefully they dress them or smartly they call them ("secularism," "humanism" or whatever), they are of no more use than the reflection Narcissus saw of himself in the water. Indeed, false gods could lead people more quickly *to* death by drowning them in the poisoned waters of their own self-absorption, just as happened to Narcissus.

So even if it is just by logic, we need the immortal to deliver us from death. That logic does not itself deliver us; it only opens us to the Deliverer. As believers in the Triune God revealed through Jesus Christ, we proclaim that death has been destroyed. Its claim to subject us to unending nothingness is denied.

Death's destruction took place in the body, blood, soul and divinity of the Son of God made man for our sake. This we need to consider soberly when we receive Holy Communion.

That he might destroy death from the inside, Jesus took on our mortal flesh, and by surrendering himself to death in sinless love for us and for the Father, he entered into and destroyed the power of hell. In the Resurrection the Father responds to the self-surrender of the Son and raises him in his human body to eternal glory.

Destroying Death from the Inside

A living faith in Jesus Christ, the Son of the living God, is the only answer to the question of death, to the fear of death, to the culture of death. Faith is the only exit from the prospect of eternal nothingness, from idolatry in all its forms, from the enslaving demands of artificial self-sufficiency.

But Jesus himself had to go through the pangs of death. Otherwise he would not have saved us in what is most intimately ours—that is, our own humanity. It follows that if we are to share in what is most intimately his—that is, his divinity truly united to our humanity—then we must approach death with the attitudes, with the certainties and above all with the love of Jesus.

Our faith in, hope in and love of Jesus give us the ability to do so. These we received the day we were baptized, even though they may often seem dormant within us. On that day we were not only cleansed of original sin but, as it were, inserted into that body, into that Jesus in that body, who died for us and rose again.

Baptism really makes us one with Christ and with each other because of him. And if it makes us one in him, then our personal suffering and dying are somehow his very own and the Church's very own. Even more importantly, his suffering and dying become ours, the Church's. Just as the Israelites passed through a corridor between the raging waters, so we in dying pass through the corridor of the death of Jesus, who protects us from the raging powers of hell and leads us to the Promised Land.

Certainly, "in the days of his flesh," Jesus too suffered the fear of death and "offered up prayers and supplications, with loud cries and tears, to the one who was able to save him from death" (Hebrews 5:7). Jesus himself said, "Now my soul is troubled" (John 12:27).

He might have gone on to say, "But shall I ask God to spare my facing and going through death? How can I? I have come for this very reason: to lead the way through the waters of death in order to bring the hosts of my Father's beloved children, the holy Church, my bride, into eternal glory."

Jesus knew the torment that awaited him, but he despised it and fixed his attention on the glory to come afterward—not just the glory of the hero who defies death to its face but the glory of the Savior and Redeemer who destroys death forever. This is the new and everlasting covenant written on our hearts: that we, by baptism and faith, by obedience and reverence, by prayer, by suffering and by weeping, become one with him in living, dying, rising and ascending into heaven.

This oneness or covenant is not just for people of one race or color but for all who will believe in him. The power and unity of the Church do not come from clever organization but from the crucified, risen and ascended Lord. Hers is a unity across time and space, a unity between heaven, earth and purgatory. It is a unity in God; it is *the* unity *of* God. This is why it can never be broken or lost, no matter what we do!

Exultant Exaltation

The Gospel of John recounts, just before the verses cited at the beginning of this essay, that some Greeks came looking for Jesus. Their search for him seems to find its goal in these glorious words of Jesus: "And I, when I am lifted up from the earth, will draw *all* people to myself" (John 12:32, emphasis mine).

Jesus perceived in the request of the Greeks a sign that his death was near and that his universal mission was already beginning to be accomplished. It would be accomplished completely through his death, a death with universal implications for the lives and deaths of every human being who has ever existed. Hence the profound yet simple truth of his words: "Unless a grain of wheat falls into the earth and dies, it remains just a single grain; but if it dies, it bears much fruit" (John 12:24).

In Jesus, death has become not just the end of mortal life. Death is not suspended in nothingness; that would be the grain that would *not* fall! Rather, death has become the effective means to a new and eternal fertility, an abundant harvest, in the general resurrection from the dead.

Jesus saw that by entering the Red Sea himself and opening up the corridor of dry ground by his death, all who followed him would be drawn in behind him and, with him, would penetrate right to the throne of God. This is, oh, so different from being drawn into the water like Narcissus!

The *kind* of death Jesus died does not just refer to his being lifted up on a cross. It also means, like the harvest, being lifted up from the grave in the Resurrection and being lifted up to heaven in the Ascension. It therefore means an eternally fruitful death, not just for himself but for all who become one with him. It is by Jesus' death that Mary would be lifted up body and soul into heaven. It is by his death that, on the last day, all who are judged as truly belonging to Christ will be lifted up to the heavenly Jerusalem.

Jesus invites us not to deny death but rather, as our mortal life proceeds, to approach it in the memory and in the strength of his own death. It was not a wasteful end to a meaningless existence but the final act of self-giving love. This death would bring abundant life and give eternal meaning to his own mortal existence, lived in passionate surrender to his "Abba!" and to us, his dear brethren and his friends.

We pray that all current wars would end soon and that no more lives would be lost. But let us learn from the tragedy of casualties and massacres how to renew our faith in the living power of our baptism. Let us learn, in the light of the gospel, how to grow in spiritual maturity as we make our way toward the wedding banquet of heaven. Let us remember that Jesus reaps for us the gift of immortality.

On Reflection

How is death viewed in the society in which we live? What forms of escapism keep people from facing the problem and the reality of death? Do I share in those?

Have I reflected in a prayerful way on the meaning of the death of Jesus? On its relevance for my personal life and death?

How might Christ's death be understood as an act of healing and of mercy?

Am I ready to die for Jesus? Am I ready to die at all? How can I best prepare now for a truly Christian death?

Why is the act of euthanasia, performed freely and calculatingly, an insult to the death of Jesus?

Why is suicide, when free and conscious, a denial of baptism?

✠

Merciful Jesus, you know when I sit and when I stand, when I live and when I will die. Deliver me from the inane fear of death. Prepare me for death by giving me the grace to live a life of self-giving to the full, that my death may also be like the dying grain that bears much fruit that will last.

Help me to see how every choice of the good and every rejection of evil is an act of dying that will lead to resurrection. By such acts may your Church proclaim your death until you come in glory and draw to yourself all those who have longed for your coming. *Kyrie, eleison.*

CHAPTER TWENTY

Saint Dismas and the King of Mercy

*But the other rebuked him, saying, "Do you not fear God,
since you are under the same sentence of condemnation?
And we indeed have been condemned justly, for we are
getting what we deserve for our deeds, but this man has
done nothing wrong." Then he said, "Jesus, remember
me when you come into your kingdom." He replied,
"Truly I tell you, today you will be with me in Paradise."*
(Luke 23:40-43)

I once had the great grace of a long meditation on the passion of the Lord. I was imagining myself to be the good thief, known also as Saint Dismas. We hear about him only in the closing moments of his life, but it is not hard to imagine that, before Calvary, he had already had some kind of distant yet growing relationship with Jesus.

He would certainly have heard about him during the previous three years, as did many other thousands. Maybe initially he dismissed Jesus as a dreamer, but he cannot have failed to have wondered about his fame for loving sinners. Undoubtedly, Dismas would have heard some of the things Jesus had said, perhaps even from his own lips. Who knows what seeds of truth and conversion had then been sown and were already sprouting deep in his heart?

Death Row Inmates

In my meditation I imagined Dismas to have passed the night in the same cell as Jesus. He would have seen the bruises on Jesus' face and body. Perhaps Jesus would have spoken to him and won his heart in the desperate intimacy shared by death row inmates. It seems likely that Jesus would have sought to evangelize him, maybe by recounting the parable of the Prodigal Son to him. Jesus may have tried to reassure him in the face of death by speaking of Paradise and of that kingdom in which Jesus would be the King of governors and priests, the King of everlasting justice and peace.

Dismas, for a few short moments, may then have been alone with Jesus after his flagellation and crowning with thorns. He would have perceived with growing and heartfelt emotion the goodness, the innocence, the tremendous holiness of this man from Nazareth. He would have intuited clearly that the condemnation Jesus received was the fruit of jealousy and hatred. He would have seen directly into those sorrowing eyes, heard the quiet weeping, seen the wounds, raw and red.

Might it be that he even tried to console Jesus, to do what little he could to bring comfort to this giant of a man who acted with the gentleness of a lamb? Could it be that from this solidarity with the suffering Christ, this sharing of words, sentiments, pain and fate, Dismas's faith in Christ as his King was born?

From that shared cell both would be fetched for the slaughter. In contrast with the previous intimacy with Jesus, Dismas most surely would have felt the pain of this rude and abrupt interruption. Yet he would, on the *via crucis*, feel his heart beat strongly in deep communion with this newfound Friend, whose mysterious majesty had transformed his soul.

The whips and jeers of the crowd would only increase his sense of oneness with Jesus, and he might well by now have preferred to be nowhere else but beside his Hero. Perhaps he was aware that he was witnessing the greatest battle ever fought at the side of the greatest King there ever was. Might he have sensed he was part of the greatest love story ever told?

With every excruciating step the soul of Dismas would perceive ever more clearly the brightest spiritual light of his life. He would be a privileged witness of the unbelievable meekness and tenderness of the Lamb of God, shown in his dying words, "Father, forgive them; for they do not know what they are doing" (Luke 23:34). Perhaps at last Dismas understood that forgiveness is the chief weapon to destroy the real enemy and at the same time to save those enslaved by it—including himself.

Dismas would have seen the woman and the beloved disciple and, aware of their pain, may well have understood that his own pain had been blessed by the company and the love of Jesus. "How wonderful it must be to have Jesus as your son or as your master!" he may have imagined. Dismas had known the wonder of being the friend of Jesus for a few hours; what then must it be to have known him three years, like John, or thirty-three, like Mary!

But in his new awareness born from his association with Jesus, Dismas must also have perceived the truth about himself more clearly: how he had wasted so much of his time, his energies, his gifts on self-seeking; how sickeningly sinful he had been; how closed he had been to the friendship of God, the law of God, the grace of God; how ungrateful, how stubborn, how stupid he had been!

Yet how wonderful that, despite all of this, Jesus was yet his Friend, his King, his Lord. And the kingdom of Jesus would be his if only he admitted his sin before the sinless Christ and asked personally for his pardon.

Dismas' Profession of Faith

And so, provoked by the insolence of the other thief, Dismas pronounces a few sentences that are like a volcanic eruption of the changes that his encounter with Jesus set in motion.

We are at times inclined to oversimplify these words of the good thief, as if they were a quick and easy sound bite, giving us all some license to live the life of Riley and escape the fiery furnace by a whisker. But the truth is that Dismas utters a few of the most profound truths of our faith. He could only have done that if his heart had undergone an incredibly powerful and even shocking revolution, prepared by those first words of Jesus he had heard and matured through suffering with him to the end.

First of all Dismas puts the record straight for the other thief: "Don't you realize how crazy you are? We have no right to be saved; we are being justly punished with death for our crimes."

This is a confession of sin: Dismas has the humility and the courage to accept responsibility for his errors, and he does it in the hearing of Jesus. Then he goes on to say, "But this man has done nothing wrong" (Luke 23:41). This phrase is a profession of faith in the sinless Christ, and it is therefore a profession of faith in his divinity, for no mere human being is without sin (Our Lady being the God-given exception, of course). Dismas may have heard this from others, but it seems more likely that he grasped it by his own perception of Jesus and his openness to the gift of faith.

Finally, Dismas professes his faith in Jesus as King and as God: "Jesus, remember me when you come into your kingdom" (Luke 23:42c). Dismas cannot possibly refer to an earthly kingdom, since both he and Jesus are at the point of death. When he says, "Remember me," he is appealing to Jesus to accept his faith in him and so to save him from the death and judgment he is about to undergo, not before men but before the Most High. In other words, Dismas is professing his faith in the resurrection of the dead.

The response of Jesus to him confirms this: "Truly I tell you, today you will be with me in Paradise" (Luke 23:43). The King of the Jews thus accepts Dismas's confession of sin, his act of faith in Jesus' own divinity and in his power to raise the dead. Our Lord thus assures him that that faith will lead him to communion with God in eternity.

The Story of Every Soul

In his encounter with Dismas Jesus fulfils in a very beautiful, personal way the meaning of his entire life: to save a person, any person, all persons from sin through his Cross and resurrection. Jesus cannot save us if we will not accept our sin —all of our sin—and show that acceptance by confessing it. For if we are sinless, we do not need to be saved. He is King of the redeemed, not of those who state that they stand in little or no need of redemption.

In a soul that denies the presence of sin or justifies it in the name of tolerance or free choice or lifestyle, Christ *cannot* be King. The truth is that the certainty of death already tells us that we are indeed in sin. If we deny our sin, death will be a doorway not to the resurrection unto life but to the permanent condition of a living death, damnation or hell.

In its essentials the story of Dismas is the story of every soul. We all live with the crimes of our sins and deserve death. We all live in suffering, but no more than Jesus, who comes to our side to suffer with us and for us so that our sins might be taken away. He asks us only to be open to his friendship, to recognize and confess our sins, to profess his sinlessness, to witness the immensity of his tenderness and compassion and to die in the sure promise that he will remember us when we stand naked at the threshold of Paradise.

On Reflection

In terms of timing, can we be sure that Dismas's conversion took place only when he was eye-to-eye with Jesus on the cross?

From the story of Dismas, what can be said to be the essential criterion for being with Jesus in Paradise?

Does the story of Dismas justify delaying conversion and confession?

How does Jesus seek to evangelize the "criminal" in me?

What would I say to Jesus if I hung beside him on the cross? What would I say to Dismas?

✠

Merciful Jesus, remember me! In remembering you I am remembered by you, so let the thought of you be ever on my mind and in my heart. Although the crime of sin hardens my heart to you, from the depths of that heart, like the Prodigal Son in the depths of his miserable exile, let me remember you and the Father's house. Grant me urgency in converting to you, without excuses, without delays, without procrastinations, because you alone are worthy every here and every now of every whisper of my love. *Christe, eleison.*

Conclusion

In the introduction to this little book, I underscored the mercy of God the Father, who reveals himself in Jesus, his only-begotten and beloved Son. To be honest, I did this above all to capture the reader's heart. Divine mercy is irresistible! However, I hope most sincerely that, after reading this book, you also will have come to understand more clearly something else: The mercy of God is inseparable from his truth. Indeed, mercy is not possible without truth, for if the truth does not reveal the tragedy of sin, how will the sinner ever seek mercy?

Resistance to the truth shows the insincerity of the one who asks for forgiveness, because the purpose of mercy is to return him again to that freedom that the truth alone can give. How can I truly desire renewed oneness with God if I deny the truth of his judgment about me?

It is a parody of repentance to pour forth tears for the mercy of the Lord when I have no intention of recognizing, never mind renouncing, my sins. Mercy is not an item of spiritual consumerism. The price of mercy is not our tears but Christ's blood. The truth of human existence is such that it is, to some degree, fundamentally opposed to the truth of the holiness and love of God. We cannot overlook this. If we do, we fail to honor both the sovereignty of God and human freedom.

The truth is that all have sinned. This lack must be somehow made up: It is just and necessary that it be so, so that people and God can again be really united. And here is the wonder of God's design: We, who of ourselves are unable to make recompense to God, are made able to do so by that man who is also God, Jesus Christ our Lord. All we need do is accept this incredible generosity of God's commitment of himself to us.

How then can we explain away, or ignore, the truth of Jesus Christ entrusted to his Church and handed on, guarded and protected in its integrity by successive generations of apostles and martyrs? We simply cannot do so. What the Church teaches us in matters of faith and morals is what Christ himself teaches.

This is our faith, and if we have legitimate questions to raise, let them be raised, not in a spirit of mundane skepticism but with a willing and heartfelt docility toward those to whom Christ has entrusted the office of teaching for our salvation's sake. These men are our fathers in Christ. Surely we owe them at least the filial respect of a son or daughter. They will not give their children stones instead of their daily bread.

Mercy will always reach the heart of the one who fails to live according to that teaching, if that heart repents with sincerity and humility. To the degree, however, that people refuse to accept that truth and know what they are doing in so refusing, the mercy of Christ will stand against them in their time of judgment, for they have closed their hearts to his truth. To refuse the truth is to refuse mercy, itself the core meaning of the sin that will not be forgiven, the sin against the Holy Spirit (see Matthew 12:31).

This is hard teaching. It demonstrates the seriousness of the Christian life, stemming from the seriousness of sin and the seriousness of Christ's suffering and death to remedy it.

Yet it is vital that we do not cheapen or weaken or misconstrue the true meaning of the mercy of God, for on that mercy depends our salvation.

At the end of this book, then, I encourage the reader to beg the Lord for a heart that is deep and true in its obedience and religious acceptance of the teaching of Christ in his Church. Further, in the certainty that proceeds from that truth, may you have invincible hope and trust in the mercy of the eternal Father, made visible in Christ Jesus our Lord.

In him mercy and truth have kissed (see Psalm 85:10).

Notes

Introduction

[1]Blaise Pascal, *Pensées, with an English Translation, Brief Notes and Introduction,* H.F. Stewart, D.D., trans. (New York: Pantheon Books, MCMXLVII).

Part One: Mercy and the Trinity

Chapter One: Being and Giving Forgiveness

[1]See the poem "Love III" by George Herbert:

> But quick-eyed Love, observing me grow slack
>> From my first entrance in,
> Drew nearer to me, sweetly questioning
>> If I lacked anything.

(Arthur M. Eastman, et al. eds., *The Norton Anthology of Poetry.* New York: W.W. Norton, 1970, p. 288.)

Part Three: Mercy and the Sacraments

Chapter Eleven: The Body of Merciful Love

[1]"Dogmatic Constitution on the Church," Documents of Vatican Council II, Chapter one, Section one. See also "The Constitution on the Sacred Liturgy," Documents of Vatican Council II, Chapter one, Section ten. www.vatican.va.

[2]Pope John Paul II, *Ecclesia de Eucharistia* (On the Eucharist in Its Relationship to the Church) (Vatican City: Libreria Editrice Vaticana), paragraph 59.

Chapter Twelve: The Bread and Breath of Life

[1]See Teresa of Avila, *Interior Castle* (New York: Image, 1972).

Chapter Thirteen: Divine Mercy

[1]Sister Faustina Kowalska, *Diary of Sister M. Faustina Kowalska: Divine Mercy in My Soul* (Stockbridge, Mass.: Marian, 1987), p. 570.

[2]Pope John Paul II, *Dives in Misericordia* (The Mercy of God), 7 (Boston: Pauline, 1980), p. 26.

[3]Kowalska, p. 1074.

[4]St. Augustine, *The City of God*, an abridged version from the translation by Gerald Walsh, S.J., et al., edited by Vernon J. Bourke. (New York: Doubleday, 1957), p. 178.

[5]*Ecclesia de Eucharistia*, p. 11.

[6]Kowalska, p. 1448.

[7]Kowalska, p. 1146.

Part Four: Mercy and Life

Chapter Fifteen: Attractive Distractions

[1]St. Jerome, "Commentaries on the Prophecies of Isaiah," *The Divine Office: The Liturgy of the Hours According to the Roman Rite, Vol. III.* (London and Glasgow: Wm. Collins; Sydney: E.J. Dwyer; Dublin: Talbot Pres, 1974), p. 301.

Chapter Nineteen: Healing Our Notion of Death

[1]See Saint Francis of Assisi, "Canticle of the Sun" in Marion Habig, ed., *St. Francis of Assisi: Omnibus of Sources*, 3rd ed. (Chicago: Franciscan Herald Press, 1973), p. 130.